"Pat Summerall's remarkable tale is a great American success story that includes all the ups and downs of real life. From the playing field to the broadcast booth, from triumph to tragedy and back again, it is an inspiring story of achievement and redemption. One of the legendary voices of sports has a great deal to say that speaks to all of us."

Paul Tagliabue, NFL Commissioner

"What a story! I know my old buddy Pat was a New York Giant, and of course, the cool, smooth voice of sports for many years. But, the new, rejuvenated Patrick Summerall's LIFE is just beginning. Now there's a story we'll all want to hear and want to cheer."

Tom Brookshier, CBS Broadcaster, Former Philadelphia Eagle

"Pat Summerall is a true gentleman that has lived a life that will inspire each of us in some way. I'm grateful that Pat is my friend and I thank him for sharing his story. It's a reminder on the importance of faith, family and friends. Pat has all three in abundance!"

Troy Aikman, Former Quarterback, Dallas Cowboys

"*Summerall: On and Off the Air* takes you on an intimate journey of Pat Summerall's life—through his triumphs and downfalls and into his heart and mind. The book is moving and honest and will endear you even more to one of sport's greatest icons."

James Brown, CBS Sports

"Pat Summerall's personal story captures the voice of American sports and tells of the grace that changed and sustained him in life's wins and losses. Pat is a true legend in sports history, and this riveting account of his life experiences will inspire as well as entertain every reader. This book is a delightful and dynamic reminder that new beginnings really are possible!"

Dr. Jack Graham, Pastor, Prestonwood Baptist Church

SUMMERALL
ON AND OFF THE AIR

PAT SUMMERALL

THOMAS NELSON
Since 1798

NASHVILLE   DALLAS   MEXICO CITY   RIO DE JANEIRO   BEIJING

Published in Nashville, Tennessee, by Thomas Nelson, Inc.

Nelson Books titles may be purchased in bulk for educational, business, fund-raising, or sales promotional use. For information, please e-mail SpecialMarkets@ThomasNelson.com.

ISBN 978-1-59555-242-6 (trade paper)

Library of Congress Cataloging-in-Publication Data

Summerall, Pat.
    Summerall : on and off the air / by Pat Summerall.
    p. cm.
    ISBN 0-7852-1492-5 (hardcover)
    1. Summerall, Pat. 2. Sportscasters--United States--Biography. I.
Title.
    GV742.42.S85A3 2006
    070.4'49796092—dc22
    [B]

                                                                  2006015617

Printed in the United States of America
08 09 10 11 12 LSI 5 4 3 2 1

To my wife, Cheri, whose love, loyalty and care
kept me alive with the desire to tell this story.

And to my three children, Susan, Jay and Kyle,
who found a way in their hearts to
re-accept me as a father.

CONTENTS

PROLOGUE

ON THE DAY AFTER THE 1992 MASTERS TOURNAMENT IN AUGUSTA, I got an unusual telephone call from my former CBS Sports broadcasting partner and drinking buddy, Tom Brookshier. He offered none of his usual jokes or invitations to party. For a change, Brookie was all business.

A Philadelphia native and former Eagle, Brookie had success in real estate dealings in his hometown after our years in the booth together at CBS. He had just launched a new endeavor in which he and former 76ers superstar Julius Irving—"Dr. J"—were marketing corporate luxury boxes at Philly's new arena, the Wachovia Spectrum.

"I've got this big corporate client and he's a huge fan of yours," he told me. "If you just come and meet this guy, I think I can ice this deal."

I told Brookie I didn't have the time to do a meet-and-greet. I was sick, tired, and way overbooked. But he persisted.

"Patrick, I really need this sale. I've never asked you for a favor like this before. Please come, even if you can only stay five minutes . . ."

There was desperation in his voice. I sensed he was struggling, and because of our long friendship, I agreed to come. But why did Brookie call me Patrick? That was always a sign of trouble.

There was something very strange about the whole scenario for this

1

meeting. Brookie asked me to come to a small hotel in Cherry Hills, New Jersey—an unusual place to wine and dine corporate bigwigs. But I went anyway—anything for my pal.

When I arrived, he met me at the door. Brookie was usually all smiles when we got together, but not this day. His greeting seemed forced. He looked grim and on edge. He guided me to the elevator, and we rode up to the twelfth floor in near silence. He then directed me to a conference room.

When Brookie opened the door, I was surprised to see a roomful of people. And the familiar faces—I knew all but one of them—also looked grim. I quickly sensed that this was an ambush: an "intervention," as it is known in certain circles. And I was the guest of dishonor.

I had an urge to bolt for the emergency exit, but Brookie guided me into the room. All fourteen people seated in the circle either were related to me or were long-time friends, except a man I figured was the ring-leader—the "interventionist."

Among those in the room were CBS president Peter Lund; PGA Tour commissioner Deane Beman; Tampa Bay Buccaneers president Hugh Culverhouse; my long-suffering wife, Kathy; a friend and former neighbor from Jacksonville Beach who was a doctor at the Mayo Clinic; a golfing buddy, Ross Tucker; a Tampa friend, Bob Cromwell; and my golf-broadcasting boss, Frank Chirkinian.

The man I did not recognize was a representative of the Betty Ford Clinic in Palm Springs. He and others were standing by to escort me to their clinic as a candidate for treatment as an alcoholic, he explained. "This is an intervention by the people who care about you," he said.

I swore at all of them and threatened to leave. I kept cursing under my breath as they told me that they had convened two days earlier out of concern for my health and welfare. Then, one by one, each person read aloud a letter he or she had written to me. In these letters, they expressed their love and affection for me, and their shared fear that I was in danger of destroying not only my reputation but my life.

In my anger, I tuned them out. *You hypocrites*, I thought. I knew some in that circle had their own addictions and dark secrets. Others, I decided, were there just to make themselves look good to their superiors. They didn't give a @%!& about me.

Yet some of what was in those letters got through the fury of my denial.

Brookshier was the last to speak. Before I could rip into my longtime drinking partner, he shut me up by saying he simply had been asked to read a letter written by my daughter, Susan, my oldest child. She couldn't be there because she couldn't leave her own children.

I hadn't been there much for my kids, but Susan's letter made it clear that I'd hurt them even in my absence. She recounted one incident after another. I was numb to most of it, sad to say. Yet her final words made my knees buckle: "Dad, the few times we've been out in public together recently, I've been ashamed we shared the same last name . . ."

My defiant mask fell away, leaving me shamed, self-disgusted, and weeping the first tears of regret I'd ever recalled shedding. To the surprise of all, I numbly gave myself over to the people from the Betty Ford Clinic.

They had a plane waiting. It was time to end my long-running boys' night out. Game called on account of drunkenness.

CHAPTER ONE

LAKE CITY

I was born on May 10, 1930, with a bum leg, into a family broken beyond repair. My parents separated while I was still in my mother's womb, and from what I would gather later, it was just as well. They wanted no part of each other, or of me.

I'd entered the world with not only a "club foot" but with my entire right leg twisted backward. Despite this inauspicious beginning, my life soon turned around and I enjoyed a very blessed existence, at least from a certain male perspective. It might have been an entirely different sort of life had my guardians just given up and left my poor defective leg alone. That was definitely a consideration. In rural Lake City, Florida, treatment options were limited and risky at best. But Dr. Harry Bates, a general practitioner, offered to try a new procedure that involved breaking my tiny contorted leg, turning it around, and resetting it.

There wasn't much hope that I'd be able to walk normally, even if all went well. They expected my right leg would always be shorter than the left one. I'd likely have a limp for the rest of my life. Still, Dr. Bates said, if something was to be done, it had to be while my little bones were still malleable. So my mother, Cristelle, consented, and a few days later, in our town's modest Lake Shore Hospital, Dr. Bates went to work to straighten me out.

As my aunt and uncle later told me, they were very worried about the experimental procedure. Since I was still an infant, only time would tell whether the operation had been successful. I spent the first six weeks of my life in a cast.

When the cast finally came off, Dr. Bates was amazed; I had turned out better than he'd dreamed possible. With therapy and a little luck, the doctor said, it was possible that someday I might walk with only a slight limp. He doubted, however, that I'd ever be able to run or play sports.

Maybe it was the breakup of their marriage prior to my birth, or maybe it was the sight of my twisted leg after I was born—for whatever reason, my real mother and father never embraced me as their child. I had no bond with my father, George Allen Summerall, who was not much of a father even when he was around. My mother took care of me for my first three years, then announced one day that she could no longer handle the responsibility. Eager to get rid of me, she'd already made plans to take me to an orphanage. To my lasting gratitude, her sister and brother-in-law, Clarice and Floyd Kennon, stepped up and offered to take me into their family, which included a built-in brother, their son, Mike, who was not quite a year older than I.

Mike and I were close in age and size, and since the Kennons were Irish, our similarities inspired references to Pat 'n' Mike, the fictional buddies whose shenanigans—which often involved drinking—were the basis for a series of popular Irish jokes in that era. The result was that, although I was named George Allen Summerall at birth, I became forever known as "Pat." The name worked out well, and so did my patched-together family.

The Kennons provided a family for me so that I never really missed having my own. My mother remarried while I was still a toddler, and she and her new husband took me back for a while, but they fought and I didn't fit into their plans. I must have blocked out most memories of my time with them, though I do recall a couple of beatings with a water hose from my stepfather.

When it became clear that I could not stay in that household, my paternal grandmother and the Kennons agreed to share responsibility for raising me. I spent a lot of time playing with Mike and hanging out at the Kennons, but mostly I lived with my widowed grandmother, who poured her love into my sad and battered bucket.

She was a classic Southern lady with a classic Southern name, Augusta Georgia Summerall. My grandfather, Thomas Jefferson Summerall, had died years before, so Grandma, who had been around children most of her life as a teacher in a one-room schoolhouse, didn't mind sharing her one-bedroom house at the corner of Seventh and Duval streets with me. We also shared her only bed, sleeping side by side all through my grade-school and high-school years in Lake City.

Northern Florida was a wonderful place to grow up, surrounded by scores of springs and lakes and rivers and swamps and woods. Lake City was originally settled near a Seminole village with a name meaning "Alligator Town." It is still an Old Florida sort of town; its thick canopy of live oaks are draped in Spanish moss, and their swooping limbs make great climbing.

We were just thirty-five miles or so from the Georgia state line. Bordered by the Suwannee River in the north and the Santa Fe River in the south, Columbia County has been referred to as "South Georgia" because of its slow-moving and genteel Southern orientation. Both rivers provided a boy with great venues for canoeing, fishing, and exploring; the surrounding Osceola National Forest was a two-hundred-thousand-acre playground of pine woods, marshes, tropical "jungle," and cypress swamps.

I don't have any idea how old my grandmother was when she took me in. She always seemed very fragile to me. She was a gentle and kind person who mothered me without babying me. I was expected to do my share of household chores from an early age. I washed my own school clothes every night because I only had two decent shirts and two pair of school pants. It was also my job to keep the coals burning in the potbelly stove that warmed the house in those chilly North Florida winters.

A GRANDMOTHER'S VOICE

I never knew my grandfather, but my grandmother often told me stories of him and other ancestors while we sat on the open front porch of her house, which served as my grandmother's neighborhood broadcast booth. I never got tired of her stories, which were frequently interrupted by greetings and conversations with people walking by. Everyone knew her as "Aunt Georgia."

These were the war years, so gas was rationed and people walked most places. It always struck me that nearly everyone who came by our house in Lake City—in fact, nearly everyone I knew—had not one but two surnames, such as Maggie Bell or Jimmy Charles.

When she wasn't chatting with passing neighbors, my grandmother would tell me the same stories about my grandfather or other ancestors over and over again without much variation, though I never grew tired of hearing them. She told me of her own childhood and memories from the Civil War era. Florida's biggest Civil War engagement, the battle of Olustee or the battle of Ocean Pond, took place just a few miles to the east. Nearly ten thousand Union and Confederate soldiers fought within just a few miles of where her family lived in the deep woods with only two other families nearby.

Since most of the men were called to war, my grandmother and her girlfriends would hide when Union soldiers came walking through. Some of the older, more aggressive women would hide in the brush, lure stragglers off the road, and then hit them over the head and steal their clothes and weapons. My grandfather, who was older than she, was captured by Yankees and imprisoned in Fort Delaware; he had to eat rats to stay alive until he became a trustee and got a job in the officers' mess hall. Then he'd steal food and hide it in the lining of his coat for himself and the other prisoners.

My grandmother's Civil War tales always mesmerized me. She'd also tell me stories of growing up in the woods with only a few other families nearby. She and her girlfriends would bathe in their old-fashioned swimsuits in a huge, hollowed-out log filled with rainwater because they had no plumbing.

My boyhood mirrored that of most Southern kids from families of limited means. My grandmother was a member of the First Methodist Church of Lake City, where I dutifully attended Sunday school until the seventh grade or so. I was supposed to attend church in high school but mostly I skipped out with friends and hit the soda fountains at the DeSoto Drug Store or the Lake City Pharmacy. The concept of God was at best an abstraction for me. Even when I did go to church, I remember wondering, *What is this all this about?* I wasn't an atheist, but faith and religion sounded like adult concepts to me. They just accounted for a very long hour or so once a week if I made it to the church at all.

By the time I got to high school, my grandmother did not have the strength to demand that I go to church. But she was a loving presence in my childhood. I grew up to the soft rhythms of her voice and to those on the radio of Fibber McGee and Molly, Amos 'n' Andy, and news and sports broadcasters from stations in Atlanta and across the Southeast. The military battles and bombs dropping in Germany, Japan, and Korea were not on my radar all that much. Like many boys my age, if I wasn't playing sports I was tuning in to a game on the radio. Even when I worked in the DeSoto Drug Store as an eighth grader, I gave most of my dusting attention to those shelves within earshot of the radio and whatever game was on.

My grandmother and I also listened to the radio as we shot marbles together on the rug. She had game, and she sometimes indulged my passion for sports in ingenious ways. She'd even haul an old straight chair off the porch, plant it in the front yard, and sit in it so we could play catch. I got to be pretty accurate throwing a baseball and football since Grandma didn't have a lot of range in that old chair. Most of the time, she'd flip or roll the ball back to me. So to practice my catching I'd find other kids, especially my cousin Mike, or I'd toss the ball up on the roof or against the house and let it bounce back. I'd do that for hour upon hour, yet Grandma never complained about the constant pounding against the house.

ALL SPORTS

My love of sports must have been part of my genetic makeup—courtesy of my mother. My father disdained all sports as a waste of time and energy, but my mother was an athlete who played basketball in high school long before girls' sports received much attention.

Yes, as long as I was bouncing or throwing a ball, I was happy. By the time I started school, I'd forgotten that my right leg was supposed to keep me from running or playing sports. The other kids never knew it either, especially since I proved to be bigger, faster, and more agile than all of my classmates—most of the older kids, too.

Though I didn't play any organized sports until the seventh grade, I spent nearly every waking hour playing or practicing or reading about sports. I had a job delivering newspapers on my bike, but my customers often got their newspapers late because I'd get absorbed reading the sports pages when I was supposed to be folding my papers for delivery.

Oddly enough, I became an avid Yankees fan, which was an strange allegiance for a Florida cracker kid to form. But the Yankees made headlines and the radio news, so I knew the Bronx Bombers line-up forward and backward. I kept up with the exploits of Joltin' Joe DiMaggio and Phil Rizzuto until they both went off to war.

When I began my freshman year in the fall of 1944 at Lake City's Columbia High School, I was determined to play every team sport they offered. Since grade school I'd been following the high school's athletic program through every season, and I couldn't wait to be a Tiger. It's a good thing I made the freshman football team, because they would have had a hard time keeping me off the field if I hadn't. At first they put me at center, though I probably weighed all of 150 pounds in full pads and helmet. Eventually they saw that I had good speed and hands so they moved me to end, both on offense and defense.

ATTITUDE ADJUSTMENT

I didn't really hit my stride as an athlete until my sophomore basketball season. I was growing fast, and for a while it seemed like I couldn't do much except stand around and watch. I was a little goofy, and I tended to be more of a spectator than a participant even when I was in the game.

The basketball coach, Jim Melton, jolted me out of my lethargic approach with a shot of tough love. He was already agitated because of a string of locker-room thefts, so when I walked into his office one day wearing a pair of gym shorts with another kid's name on them it set him off.

"Where did you get those shorts?" he demanded.

I told him I'd found them on the floor. That earned me a slap in the chops.

"Get those shorts off, Summerall," he said. "And while you're here, I wanna talk to you about something else. You're the tallest guy I've got, and all you do is pass the ball and stand around. I need somebody who can shoot the ball and stick it in the hole—and I need somebody to start getting rebounds. Step up your intensity and change your attitude, or you'll spend every game on the bench."

That brief moment would probably result in school board hearings and lawsuits today. But with that single slap and a few sharp words, Coach Melton turned a spectator into a player. I went from being passive to demanding the ball and controlling the game. It was as if Coach Melton had flipped a switch that connected my love and knowledge of sports with my natural instincts as an athlete. It had seemed like I didn't know what to do with myself before our little talk. After his wake-up call, things began clicking for me, and my confidence grew almost as rapidly as my body.

SELF-TAUGHT ACE

During my freshman and sophomore years of high school I concentrated on team sports in school, but a sports sideline that I picked up in the neighborhood also helped my athletic development. Tennis wasn't exactly the game of choice for most poor, small-town Southern kids back then, but my grandmother's house was close to Young's Park, the town's only public park. It had two tennis courts, and when I was about ten years old and bored with bouncing the ball off the house, I started wandering over there to watch people playing tennis.

It wasn't a big sport around town—mostly older guys trying to get some exercise. Sometimes they'd show up alone, hoping to find someone to hit balls with them, and I'd come running out of the house to volunteer. Usually I had to borrow a racket. The high school didn't even have a team, and there were only a couple of other kids who could hit the ball over the net with any regularity. But it was a sport and it involved a ball, so I was up for it.

If I wasn't playing sports I was reading about them in the newspapers or listening to them on the radio, so I picked up some knowledge of tennis that way, too. I read about Don Budge and Bobby Riggs and other top players of the day, and I checked out books on tennis at the library to learn the finer points. I tried to drag my cousin Mike onto the tennis court, but he wasn't interested. So I played the older guys and gave them all they could handle; I was speedy and I had a strong serve. My junior year I got to be so good that my school entered me as their sole participant in the conference tournament. I was paired against guys who had played the game much longer than I, but I breezed through the tournament anyway.

There wasn't much tennis competition in northern Florida. Most of the higher-ranked players in my region were much smaller than I, and not especially quick. The bigger, faster kids generally stuck with the major sports where there was more glory. I played every sport I could; if I'd had a pony I probably would have tried polo and steeplechase, too.

HITCHHIKING RACQUET

I was so competitive and focused on sports that, after winning the conference title, I hitchhiked 360 miles to the state tennis tournament in Fort Lauderdale. Everybody thought I was nuts for even going because there were a lot of serious tennis players in southern Florida, but I was determined to go. There was no school bus to take me, and my grandmother couldn't drive me, so I packed up my stuff and stuck out my thumb with a tennis racquet tucked under my arm. Hitchhiking was more common in those days of gas shortages and fewer cars. People were also more willing to pick up hitchhikers, which was a good thing for me. I managed to get rides quickly, and a couple of the drivers even fed me, too.

I made it to Fort Lauderdale and the tournament with time to spare. I got warmed up and then whipped through the preliminary rounds. I lost the championship match, but I did take home the runner-up trophy, which I held up in one hand as I hitched my way back home.

I came into my own as an athlete in my junior year. At six feet four inches I finally stopped growing taller and was able to get comfortable with my height and put on a few pounds of muscle. Tennis had really helped my agility, and I'd toughened up enough to make the all-conference football team.

Basketball was still my favorite sport, and that year we went to the state tournament after some great games against our biggest rivals in the Northeast Conference, including Live Oak, Ocala, and Tallahassee-Leon. Our most intense rival was Live Oak, another small town in north Florida just twenty-six miles away. We played them in every sport so we had plenty of opportunities to get competitive. We even had a traveling trophy with them, an old oak bucket. It wasn't much to look at, but we beat each other silly trying to hang on to it.

I played forward alongside four senior starters, and their experience made me a better player. I was the team's leading scorer, and a few college scouts came around to see if I was worth recruiting. We dominated most of our opponents, lost only a couple games, and beat Vero Beach for the state championship. I was named to the all-state basketball team, which at that time was just about the greatest thing I could imagine.

HIGH EXPECTATIONS

It felt like a blessed life to me. I had a lot of good buddies, and even though my own father and mother never came to my games, it seemed like everyone else in town did. My uncle was there for me, and a lot of other men in town were also supportive. Some even had me over for dinner with their families to talk sports.

Frank Oosterhoudt, my friend Sam's father, was a wealthy lumberman who treated me like another son, giving me a quarter a week on top of the dime I got from my own family. The town druggist was another supporter; he paid us ten cents a point for scoring in basketball games. That was big money back when movies cost nine cents and you could get a soda for a nickel.

My cheerleader girlfriend and good buddy Bettye Beban was an even better reward for being a local sports hero. She was dark-haired, quiet, and one of the prettiest girls in our school. She was also one of the smartest students, which was an added benefit since my grades needed all the help they could get. I struggled to stay eligible for sports both because of my poor grades and because I had a certain tendency to create mischief in and out of school.

Mine were mostly small-town, juvenile pranks: stealing pies out of the home economics kitchen, looking through peepholes into the girls' locker room, putting garbage cans in the middle of the street, and throwing tomatoes at cars. I wasn't into drinking in high school, though a few of my teammates were known to do it. It just didn't appeal to me then, probably because their cocktail of choice involved mixing cheap wine and Coca-Cola. One taste of that concoction was enough to make a guy swear off booze for life.

I made the all-conference and all-state teams in football and basketball in my senior year, though we didn't win any state titles. Columbia High fielded its first baseball team that year, too. I played first base and did pretty well, which was a good thing since people had come to expect me to be good at every sport.

As the town's leading athlete, there were high expectations about my college career. Most folks were pushing me to become a Gator at the University of Florida, just fifty-six miles south of Lake City. And though he had shown little interest in most aspects of my life, my father came up with the notion that I should go to the United States Military Academy at West Point. I think he liked the idea of me being disciplined by tough-guy drill sergeants, since his own efforts had mostly failed.

COLLEGE VISITS

In his continuing campaign to set me straight, my father kept pushing me to go to West Point. I even agreed to go to New York State for a campus visit with him. But my initial and lasting impression was that the Academy looked way too much like the Florida State Penitentiary. I wasn't enthused, especially when they told me that to meet West Point's academic entrance requirements I'd have to spend my freshman year at a military school in Kentucky to get my grades up.

I had much more appealing options. I was being actively recruited by a number of good schools, including the University of Florida, which was my first choice. But I had my heart set on continuing as a multisport athlete, and the Gators football coaches made it clear that they were only tolerating my desire to play basketball. They wanted football to be my priority. I could see that it was going to be a sore point, so I began looking around for a school that would let me play both sports without haranguing me.

I'd developed a strong interest in the University of Kentucky because of their famed basketball coach, Adolph Rupp. I passed the first test when I visited the Kentucky campus in Lexington. I had to duck to go through Rupp's office door, which was only six foot two inches tall—an inch lower than his height requirement for recruits.

The coaching staff at Kentucky said they were willing to offer me a scholarship for basketball, but they weren't enthusiastic about my desire to play football, too.

"We don't think you are that talented," Rupp said.

So I turned around and ducked out the door of the man who became one of the most winning basketball coaches in NCAA history.

CHAPTER TWO

RAZORBACK

BY THE SPRING OF MY SENIOR YEAR, MY COLLEGE OPTIONS WERE narrowing quickly thanks to my stubborn insistence on playing both football and basketball. My lack of interest in schoolwork didn't help, either. Alabama, Georgia Tech, and Vanderbilt had all expressed interest in me—but my grades weren't good enough to get into those schools.

Then, in the spring of 1948, the University of Arkansas dispatched three coaches to Lake City in search of fresh talent. They gave tryouts to three of us in the senior class. One member of this coaching contingent, Razorbacks line coach Hobert Hooser, had been a highly regarded coach at my high school a few years before I got there. He was still well regarded in Lake City, and my father was one of his admirers. Even though my father had little interest in sports, he knew and respected Hooser as a disciplinarian. Since I was beginning to worry about where I would wind up the following year, I went all-out in my tryout for him and the other coaches, and they seemed to be impressed. My buddy Bobby Kinard and another teammate, Vance Roberts, also made good impressions.

Arkansas offered both Bobby and me football scholarships and said I could play basketball, too. This time my father and all the other adults in my life were on board because they figured Coach Hooser would straighten me out academically and keep me out of trouble. I was thrilled, especially since Arkansas was on a roll in football. They'd gotten bowl invitations the two previous years, tying LSU in the Cotton Bowl before winning the Dixie Bowl the following year. I signed on the dotted line to become a "Hog" on full scholarship.

The coaches said they wanted us on campus in Fayetteville by mid-August so we could get settled in before football practice started. It was tough to leave my friends and family, especially my grandmother who was in poor health, but I was ready to go. The thought of playing sports all the time on a campus full of beautiful Southern girls made it a little easier to leave my girlfriend and buddies behind, too.

It was one thousand miles from Lake City to Fayetteville, in the Arkansas Ozarks, but I soon felt at home. I didn't have to worry about being considered a small-town redneck in that environment. We arrived in time for both the fall semester and the smothering humidity of August, but I was about to experience my first genuine sampling of the other three seasons. The coaches advised those of us who weren't schol-ars that the education curriculum might be a good bet if we wanted to remain eligible for the team. So I declared myself an education major.

I had promised myself, my family members, and Coach Hooser that I'd hit the books and go to class, and I had every intention to live up to those promises. But practicing and playing two sports—and enjoying the social rewards of being a college athlete—forced me to scale back on my grade targets. I lowered my aim from "good" grades to "good enough to stay eligible" grades. Suffice it to say, my name never made it to the dean's list during my four years at Arkansas.

TALENTED TEAM

I did get quite an education in football just from hanging out with an incredible group of athletes. The Razorbacks didn't have any great seasons while I was on campus, but it wasn't because we lacked the talent. We had a bunch of guys who made it to the pros, including Fred Williams—a four-time Pro Bowl defensive tackle for the Chicago Bears who also played for the Washington Redskins. Our quarterback, Lamar McHan, and running back, Lew Carpenter, each played ten years in the NFL. One of my best buddies, Floyd Sagely, played defensive back for three seasons with the 49ers and Cardinals. Linebacker Bob Griffin put in five seasons with the Los Angeles Rams, and halfback Buddy Sutton did a stint with the Baltimore Colts.

Another standout was my roommate, defensive tackle Dave "Hawg" Hanner from Gesik, Arkansas. Hawg was my best buddy and a source of amusement for years to follow. He was a very entertaining, big-hearted guy. None of us were very sophisticated, of course, but Hawg enjoyed playing the backwoods good ol' boy, and he was very convincing in that role. He slept with a chaw of tobacco in his mouth, and every morning he'd leave a big brown circle on his pillow.

You don't expect a lot of social grace from a guy named Hawg. Besides, he was a good and true buddy who took me home with him for the shorter holidays since I lived so far away. As soon as we'd get to his house, he'd drop his suitcases on the ground and start fighting both of his "little" brothers to prove he was still top dog. Hawg weighed 280, and his brothers were in the same weight class, but he always whipped them when I was around.

We had another ritual for my visits to his house. We'd usually get a couple local girls and go driving and drinking in the woods in his pickup truck, but we always had to save a couple of shots at the bottom of the bourbon bottle for his mother. When we got home, Ma Hanner would want us to check in so she could see what kind of shape we were in, and then she'd polish off the bourbon for us.

Hawg went on to a thirteen-year career with the Green Bay Packers, and later worked as an assistant coach in the pros. But he had an even tougher time than I did with academics at Arkansas, in part because he found attending class to be an inconvenience. He even flunked a physical education course in volleyball that we were both taking.

He claimed he was going to beat up the instructor, but since Hawg had never gone to class he didn't know the teacher's name. And I refused to tell him.

UNDERACHIEVERS

We were a tight bunch, with our own fraternity of sorts. We all lived in Razorback Hall, the athletic dorms that were set apart from other student housing. In some ways, we never felt like a part of the regular college scene because we spent so much time living and playing with our teammates. Eleven guys in my class alone were offered pro contracts during our final year, so we were serious about our football, if nothing else.

Our coach, John Barnhill, was in his third season when I arrived on campus. It seemed like he had turned the football program around. He'd rallied the state around the Hogs, expanded Razorback Stadium, and taken the team to bowl games in 1946 and 1947. He'd also done a heck of a job as a recruiter. But by my sophomore year, he seemed distracted and tired. Coach Barnhill was also serving as athletic director, and all the responsibility seemed to weigh on him.

We simply were not good at a lot of the basic football skills. Our coaches seemed to feel that we had so many good players that they didn't need to focus much on fundamentals. On top of that, our game strategies seemed outdated compared to those of our opponents.

Coach Barnhill quit after my sophomore year, and they brought in Otis Douglas. He'd been successful at a couple of smaller schools and then as an assistant with the Philadelphia Eagles. Still, we just never came together as a team under him. One problem was that we split games between Little Rock and Fayetteville, which meant we never felt like the home team at either place. Still, our greatest problem is that we never found an identity as a team. It was too bad, because we had so many great athletes during my time there, including one who was in the wrong sport.

OFF COURSE

I could never figure out how a slightly built, five foot nine inch guy with a squeaky voice got a football scholarship to Arkansas, and after a few practices I think Miller Barber wondered, too.

No doubt he was an athlete. Miller had been an all-state guard on his high-school football team, where his quickness, smarts, and pure grit kept him from being creamed by bigger opponents. Still, just a couple weeks into our freshman practices, it became clear that my new buddy was in over his head at a major football school.

Every Tuesday we had to scrimmage the varsity; to them, we were tackling dummies with legs. Basically, they kicked our rear ends up and down the field once a week. It was a rite of passage for every freshman football player, climbing the steep Hill of Doom to those Tuesday practices. As we went up that first time—and every time thereafter—most of us prayed that we wouldn't come back down on a stretcher.

The varsity guys whupped on us from the first snap in our first scrimmage against them. After a couple of initial plays, we didn't want to break our huddle. Miller Barber was game, but he looked like fresh-cut meat. I looked down the huddle, and my little buddy was bent double, with his hands on his knees. Blood was dripping from the corner of his mouth and down his face. Some of it was caked on his facemask. We were all wondering if he was going to collapse before the huddle broke when he slowly raised his head and offered a squeaky surrender: "I don't know about the rest of you guys, but I'm gonna find me another sport!"

That was the last day Miller Barber played college football; he joined the Razorback's golf team and put his athletic skills to good use without having to worry about getting the crap beaten out of him every Tuesday. He became a collegiate star, made the pro tour in 1958, and went on to win eleven PGA tour events. I never again saw him with blood and mud on his face, only suntan oil and, occasionally, a little sand.

KICKING IT

The varsity guys managed to intimidate us the first couple of practices. After that we realized we had more talent, and we were just as tough. We held our own against them and had a great season against our opponents. As I recall, we didn't lose a game. I played both ways and was the leading receiver on offense, but we didn't throw all that much from our single wing offense. I was in hog heaven and I don't remember being a bit homesick. The only time I missed Lake City was when I got my first taste of an icy Ozark winter. I didn't have any winter coat, so I went to Coach Barnhill and told him that I was going home unless he could find one for me.

He sent me to a young member of the board of regents, Jackson T. "Jack" Stephens, a native of Pratt, Arkansas, who had built one the largest investment banking companies in the country and was a major benefactor at the university. Jack took me to Dillard's department store and got me my first winter coat. That began a friendship that covered many years and a lot of fairways. Jack, who was always listed in Forbes as one of the nation's wealthiest men, became only the fourth chairman of the board in the history of Augusta National. Our friendship flourished in its later years.

After the beating I took during my first season of college football, I was really looking forward to basketball. I played quite a bit my freshman year, then I moved up to the varsity squad in my sophomore year and spent more time on the bench. By the time I made the transition from football to basketball, I was behind on the learning curve. So I decided to shelve basketball to concentrate on football, which turned out to be a good move.

In my sophomore season, I developed a whole new specialty. As a kid I'd played around at field goal kicking and punting during practices, but never in a game. As it turns out, I had a knack for it—despite the fact that my right leg is a bit shorter than my left. Since I was playing both offense and defense at Arkansas, it hadn't occurred to me to volunteer my services as a kicker, too, but at the start of my sophomore year, we needed one. After a practice, one of the coaches announced that they were going to hold tryouts for a kicker the next day. I gave it a shot, just to see if I could do it, and, to my surprise, I boomed a couple of kicks sixty yards or more and won the job hands down.

I became the team's primary kickoff and field goal man, but back then teams didn't attempt many field goals. My success at kicking was just something I took in stride, so to speak. I didn't think much about the fact that it was a pretty unusual development, considering that my right leg had to be broken and turned around after I was born. I had come to take my athleticism and the good things that came with it for granted.

I did get news that made me stop and think about the woman who had always been my champion—even when my own father and mother didn't care to come to my games. I should have known that when my father called it would not be with good news. My grandmother had died. She'd been failing for a long time, and she went peacefully, he said. The funeral date was set, but he told me that I shouldn't try to come. It was a long trip. I would have had to miss classes and practices. He didn't say so, but I don't think my father had the extra money to pay my way home.

I thought about going anyway. It bothered me to not be there for her. She had been there for me, always. She was the one person whose love I never questioned. I still wish that I'd found a way to go to her funeral, but my father discouraged it and I didn't want to make waves at a time of sadness.

MINOR LEAGUER

My sports calendar kept getting longer and longer. The summer before my junior year, I got a tryout with the St. Louis Cardinals organization, even though I hadn't played any baseball since I was a senior in high school. They called and said they were always looking for good athletes. I tried out, and they put me on the roster for their Class C minor league team in Lawton, Oklahoma. There was no concern about ruining your college eligibility because you didn't get paid. You just showed up and played.

Among my teammates in Lawton were twin sluggers Roy and Ray Mantle. Their brother, Mickey, was playing with Joplin in the Class C Western Association, and we had a few games against him that summer. Like his brothers, Mickey was a rough-edged, straight-talking Okie, but on the playing field he had no equal. Even at nineteen he was a powerful switch-hitter with incredible speed. Though he was prone to fielding errors at that point, he had the aura of a star already.

I got to know Mickey through his brothers, but none of his aura rubbed off on me. After that season, it was clear that I was not cut out for major league baseball. I might have had a chance if they'd outlawed the curve ball, but that didn't appear to be a possibility. My minor league coach gave me his assessment without sugarcoating it. "If you've still got a chance to play college football next season, you probably ought to go ahead and do it," he said.

I took his hint. After my brief brush with pro baseball, I returned to Fayetteville for what turned out to be a dismal football season in my junior year. We won only two games and lost eight. Texas A&M drubbed us

42–13, and Tulsa beat us by fifteen points. Our only moral victory was a one-touchdown loss to SMU, a team led by Kyle Rote, the most amazing athlete any of us had ever seen. He later became a good friend, and I even named one of my sons after him.

COURTSIDE CALL

I'd always thought basketball was my best sport—I'd been all-state twice in that sport in high school. However, my versatility seemed to make me more suited for football. By the time my senior season rolled around, life was good in Fayetteville. I had a steady but never-too-serious girlfriend, Cherry Talbot, a fun-loving brunette from Mountain Home, Arkansas, who wound up marrying one of my roommates, quarterback Jim Rhinehart from Frederick, Oklahoma. I also felt like I was pulling my share of the load for the football team, playing both offense and defense and handling all the kicking duties.

We had a promising start to our senior football season, winning our first two games of the year in blowouts against Oklahoma State and Arizona State. But somehow we got derailed the next two weeks. We dropped close games to TCU and Baylor before going into a face-off with the fourth-ranked ranked Texas Longhorns the next week at home. Arkansas had never beaten the Longhorns at Fayetteville, and the stands were packed with thousands of hopefuls. We trailed until late, but finally broke through when I kicked a late field goal for a 16–14 win, setting off a celebration that lasted for days and cemented my place in Razorback football history.

We also hoped that this victory would give us necessary momentum for our first winning season, but then lowly Santa Clara University, a small Jesuit school in California, staged an upset and sent us into another tailspin. We lost two of the next three—including a forty-point shellacking by

Southern Methodist University—and effectively played ourselves out of both the conference race and any shot at a postseason bowl game.

When I walked off the field after my last game—a narrow victory over Tulsa in which I had kicked my final college field goal—I was a little down. I feared that my playing days might be over. However, I'd had a good year on both sides of the line, and there was talk that my kicking might attract attention from pro teams in the spring draft because I'd led the nation in field goals that year—with just four of them. Today, of course, it's not unusual for a college kicker to have four field goals in a single game.

Just as I was starting to fear that I was an over-the-hill college jock, Arkansas's basketball coach, Presley Askew, gave me a surprise call. Injuries and eligibility issues had pared the ranks of his team, so he asked if I'd help fill out the roster. I still loved basketball, so I signed on and served as the eighth man for the 1951–52 season. I got to play in some key situations, but it was tough to get into a rhythm coming off the bench, especially since I hadn't played basketball competitively for nearly two years. Still, the coach must have liked something I did because he asked me to stick around for another season. I still had a year of basketball eligibility left since I'd only played three seasons at that point. It was a sweet offer. He said I could keep my scholarship while focusing on just one sport, and I could also pick up some free grad-level courses along with my education degree.

PRO DRAFT

But then the Lions showed up at my door. Just as I was gearing up for one final fling at college basketball, the Detroit Lions made me their fourth-round pick in the 1952 NFL draft. I couldn't pass up the offer to play for the pros, even though it was for blue-collar pay back in those days.

Detroit general manager Russ Thomas—a former Lions player—said he was coming to Fayetteville to sign me. He gave me the impression that I'd already made the team and that a sizeable contract was guaranteed. That triggered delusions of grandeur and several long nights of partying at our favorite bar, Hog's Heaven, where I foolishly ordered round after round on my tab. That's where Thomas found me when he came to the campus. I was playing pinball in my usual style, with the machine's legs propped up on my toes, trying to cheat it out of some free games. I guess Thomas must have decided that was a challenge for our negotiations because he proceeded to play me like a pinball. He said that all Lions players took the same salary—$5,000 a year—as a show of team unity.

"There are no stars, and no jealousy," he said.

I thought that sounded more like a vow of poverty than unity and told him so.

The Lions' GM was not moved by my appeal.

I then countered that I'd heard that some of my teammates who'd been drafted were getting signing bonuses.

"We don't give signing bonuses," Thomas said.

He told me that if they gave me any more than the standard offer they'd have to raise the salaries of everyone on the team.

I stood my ground as best I could. I did not believe that big-name NFL stars like the Lions' Doak Walker, Bobby Layne, and Leon Hart were willing to take the same measly salary as a rookie who hadn't played a down yet.

Tiring of his human pinball game, Thomas finally upped his offer to $6,000.

I gave one final push and received for my effort a $500 signing bonus. To this day I can remember the thought that hit me when he tossed out that figure: *At least it'll pay off my bar tab.*

CHAPTER THREE

GOING PRO

WHEN I CALLED MY DAD TO TELL HIM I HAD BEEN OFFERED $6,000 TO play football, he surprised me. For a guy who'd never seemed to care about my athletic career, he almost sounded impressed.

"They're going to give you $6,000 for playing something?" he asked.

"Yes, Dad, this is professional football, so they pay you," I said.

"It doesn't sound like work to me," he replied. "But if they want to pay you that kind of money for playing something, I think you ought to take it."

My dad was still working as a janitor, and his take on my job with the Lions gave me a fresh perspective. But on the flight to Detroit it really sunk in, particularly as we approached the city, which at that point in my life seemed bigger than any place I'd ever been. For all of the talk of gridiron glory in college football, I'd led a pretty sheltered life at Arkansas. I lived, slept, ate, and played with other athletes, most of whom were small-town guys like me. It was overwhelming to think that now I was being paid to play football in a far more sophisticated city like Detroit. I only had to look down at my feet to remind myself that I was still a country boy. I had on my only pair of "good" shoes, a pair of beat-up loafers with sponge soles.

I'd been given directions for the Lions' training camp in Ypsilanti, so after grabbing my suitcase and a duffle bag, I took a cab—another unfamiliar experience—and drank in the gritty scenery of the Motor City and the suburbs where its autoworkers slept. It looked like a place where people earned every penny they were paid.

I arrived in Detroit to begin my pro football career as the first Corvette was being drawn up on a design board. President Harry S. Truman was in the White House. Our military was still trying to bomb its way out of Korea. And the National Football League, which had been struggling for a decade, was still trying to get established when many of the best athletes were off fighting wars. Television audiences were just beginning to tune in to pro football teams, but some teams still couldn't make a go of it and were forced to shut down for lack of interest. In the off-season most players worked to support their families; during the season they worried about having their eyes gouged out (at that time football helmets had no facemasks).

There wasn't much glamour in the game overall, but there was a sense that better times were ahead for both the country and the sport. Detroit's auto factories were gearing up for all those returning soldiers, the families they were starting and the wealth they were generating. The Motor City also had one of the best teams, with some of the league's marquee players. When I got to the team hotel, the staff and a lot of other people were respectfully watching a confident-looking guy standing at the reception desk. Square-jawed and muscular, he looked like a Hollywood version of a professional football player, but he was the real thing. The hotel clerk all but bowed while handing him his thick packet of fan mail. Later I found out he was Bobby Layne, the Lions star quarterback and team leader. But I didn't have to know his name to understand that this was a guy who, like Detroit, only gave you what you earned.

ROOKIE RITUALS

I was feeling good about becoming a pro, but meeting a bonafide star like Layne made me realize that I hadn't yet earned that level of respect. Among my teammates I was just an unproven rookie, only slightly higher in rank than a ball boy. Two younger veterans—Leon Hart, the All-American back from Notre Dame, and safety/halfback Jack Christiansen—helped me get settled in, which I appreciated. But their friendship didn't spare me from the traditional rookie hazing, including being forced to stand and sing the Arkansas fight song during daily meals at the training table. I was no Frank Sinatra, and it didn't help that I had never learned all the words to my own school song. My embarrassment brought roars of delight from Lions' veterans, who made certain I performed at every meal.

Rookies learned to take the hazing in stride or face consequences that were far worse. It helped us bond with our teammates, particularly those of us just trying to make the team. Shortly after arriving at training camp, I learned that my contract was not guaranteed. I was also straightened out on the disparity in salaries. As I'd suspected, GM Russ Thomas had played me for a rube when he told me that everyone on the team made the same salary. Back then, players' salaries were not subject to media scrutiny, and most players didn't have agents pushing for top dollar. We didn't even get paid for preseason exhibition games.

I learned that the star veterans like Layne made considerably more than the rest of us. Most players lived in cheap suburban hotels during the season. Some of the guys, especially those with families, were barely making it. Even the team's top draft pick that year, University of Texas guard Harley Sewell, was so hard-pressed for cash that he couldn't afford a decent suit. Bobby Layne, also a Texas grad, stepped up to help out the rookie. Our snappy-dressing quarterback paid a tailor to measure Sewell for a couple of new suits to uphold the Longhorn image.

Layne took his role as team captain seriously. He was a superior athlete who'd also been a record-setting pitcher for the University of Texas base-ball team. But it was his competitiveness, focus, and drive that set him apart as a natural leader, and that the other great players admired. Layne had joined the Lions in 1950 and immediately helped to turn the franchise around. He expected each of us to play with his intensity.

Despite my best efforts, I got on his bad side during an exhibition game against the Philadelphia Eagles. On third down, I set up at tight end after Coach Buddy Parker called a pass play to me. Unfortunately, I got knocked down at the line. Layne went back to pass but couldn't find me on the field so he had to eat the ball and take a sack—an outcome guaranteed to put a quarterback in a foul mood.

After the offensive series ended, I went to the sidelines where I heard Layne taking my name in vain because of the busted play. He made sure I heard him as he told the coach: "That Bozo never got off the line. Don't ever put him on the field when I'm in the game."

It was the sort of thing that rookies heard a lot from veterans in the heat of battle. I knew Layne would get over it, and he did. But before I earned his respect and friendship, I had to learn to fight off defenders at the line and to run my pass patterns as they were diagrammed in prac-tice. He got a lot friendlier once I showed that I could get to the right place at the right time, catch the ball, and move it toward the goal line. It wasn't that the pros hit me any harder than I'd been hit in college. The game was just much faster, and the players were smarter in their approach to the fundamentals. There were tricks and techniques that rookies had to master if they had any hope of matching up against the more seasoned pros. Once I proved that I was trainable, Layne and the other veterans and coaches warmed up considerably.

I tried to make myself useful by playing both ways and doing some kicking, too. Most guys were two-way players because NFL teams only had thirty-three man rosters. We had a lot of guys who could kick as a sidelight. Fullback/linebacker Pat Harder did most of the placekicking, but Layne could kick, as could Walker and linebacker Jim Martin. As a rookie, I was last in line to get practice kicks. Once I showed the strength of my kicking leg, I did most of the kicking off, but I only got the call on field goals if it was forty yards or more.

FITTING IN

In an early exhibition game against the Chicago Cardinals, I had the usual rookie jitters. But something clicked and I had a great day on both offense and defense. A few days later, we were going over the game film after practice and the coach complimented a block I made on the punt return. Actually, the film was so grainy he couldn't tell it was me at first, but he pointed to my body on the screen and said, "That's a hell of a block."

He ran it again and still couldn't tell who the blocker was, so he asked us. Still a little nervous, I sheepishly raised my hand.

"Great job!" the coach said.

That was music to a rookie's ears, but I received an even greater compliment after practice when Layne invited me to join his social circle for a visit to his favorite jazz club in Detroit. He proved to be every bit as intense in his recreational pursuits as he was on the field. We stayed late into the night, with Layne laying out heavy tips to hear his favorite sax man play "Night Train" over and over.

Layne, who was known to puff cigarettes on the sidelines, was the leader of the Lions "Rat Pack," a free-spirited bunch who would go out for drinks and buck curfew. He was my teammate, but I was as starstruck as a fan around him. The fact that he even knew my name was a thrill. I admired the fact that he played and partied with equal intensity, and I did my best to emulate him in both regards.

SIDELINED

Just as I was starting to feel at home with the Lions and in the league, I pulled a hamstring running a simple pass pattern. I'd never been hurt before. It felt like a betrayal when pain shot through my leg and I came up lame. The worst thing I'd ever had in college was a blister. With this injury, my whole leg turned black and blue, and I could hardly walk.

That night I stood in the shower for hours, letting hot water soothe the soreness and enhance the blood flow in my leg. I'd taken my healthy body for granted throughout my playing days; this was a whole new deal for me. Instead of realizing how lucky I'd been and taking this injury in stride, I cursed my bad luck. I couldn't practice for ten days, and I felt like I was losing ground. I still hadn't officially made the team, so I was worried and depressed until I got the nod from the team's tailor. It was a bit of an anticlimax, but it beat being handed a plane ticket home.

Like most pro teams back then, the Lions made their players wear matching dress suits on road trips. So when Larry Gersh, the team tailor, stopped by my locker to make an appointment for a fitting, I knew I'd made the cut despite my hamstring injury. Any further doubts were dispelled when the equipment manager informed me that he'd ordered a pair of square-toed kicking shoes for me. It wasn't a brass band and a million dollar bonus, but I was glad to take it.

My hamstring healed in time for the opening game of my first NFL season, which ended without glory in a fourteen-point loss to the San Francisco 49ers. Then I got a lesson in the cruel realities of professional sports. Things were looking much better in our second game, this one against our primary NFL West rivals, the Los Angeles Rams. We were up by three points on their home field late in the fourth quarter.

On the last play of the game, I was rushing Rams quarterback Norm Van Brocklin as he faded back to launch a desperation pass to receiver Elroy "Crazy Legs" Hirsch. I saw Rams fullback Paul "Tank" Younger running toward me, but before I could make a move on him, somebody came out of nowhere and cut-blocked me. I stuck out my right arm to break my fall just as Younger dove at me. He blasted my arm just as it made contact with the ground, sending a lightning bolt of pain through it.

Van Brocklin's pass fell incomplete and my teammates celebrated. I didn't join the victory dance. My arm was numb; I knew Tank had done some serious damage to it. I tried to find the team doctor in the mass of people jogging off the field, but settled for a trainer.

He rolled back my jersey sleeve and revealed a sickening sight. Bones were protruding through the skin of my upper arm.

"It looks like a compound fracture. We'd better get you to a hospital," he said.

They put me in an ambulance as everyone else was showering and preparing to fly back to Detroit. It was a tricky break, so the doctors had to operate immediately. Afterward, they kept me in an L.A. hospital for nearly a week. The pain in my arm wasn't nearly as bad as the agonizing I did over my career.

It didn't get any better when I returned to Detroit. I slipped and fell down some stairs, compounding the compound fracture. More pain. Another operation. This time, doctors put pins inside each bone with little hooks sticking out, so the pins could be removed. Then they put my arm in a big cast and sent me home. My rookie year had ended before it could really get going. I didn't return to the sidelines until the Thanksgiving Day game, and even then I was just a spectator, watching my teammates get an impressive win over Green Bay.

PAYDAY

While I recuperated and sulked, the Lions set about proving that they didn't need my services. They went on a roll, winning eight of their last nine games to tie the Rams for the Western Conference lead. That forced a home playoff game for the league championship. The Lions won that, too, and then beat the Cleveland Browns 17–7 to win the NFL title. This was before the days of the Super Bowl, so it was not a global event; just the same, I felt badly about not contributing to the team's successful season. They didn't hand out those enormous NFL Championship rings in those days either, but I did get a nice championship jacket and, even better, a little something extra in the last paycheck of the season.

My championship bonus inspired me to put down $3,000, about half a year's salary, on a flashy new Olds 88. It was turquoise with a red Naugahyde interior. I drove it off the dealership lot and all the way home to Lake City. I rolled into town looking sharp, even if I felt a little sheepish about missing most of the season because of my injury. I got over the sheepish part by buying several rounds for my buddies, then taking them for a spin in my hot new wheels.

"@%!&, they don't pay you that much, do they?" one asked upon seeing the Olds.

"Why, yes they do," I was happy to reply.

But my injury had reminded me that I couldn't count on that NFL paycheck for the rest of my life. So a few weeks later I did something that not many pro athletes did in their off-season: I reenrolled at Arkansas for spring semester graduate classes. I still had a lot of friends on campus, including my old roommate and running buddy Hawg Hanner, who was trying to make up for lost—or simply abandoned—study time after his first season with the Green Bay Packers.

SUMMER SCHOOL

It wasn't Hawg, or even one of my female friends, who inspired me to return to campus. My frail, gray-haired history teacher, Mr. Dorsey Jones, succeeded in motivating me when many teachers before him had failed. He had inspired me with his brilliance. His eloquent lectures were as engrossing as great novels. He taught a number of history courses, and I'd tried to take every one available to undergraduates. My favorite courses with him were in Russian history, so I decided to pursue that as a graduate degree. He made the topic, and everything he taught, so fascinating that I earned straight A's in his classes while barely pulling C's and D's in everything else.

Hawg and I purchased an extra campus car, a 1935 Ford for $35, just because we could. There was only one thing wrong with the car: it lacked air conditioning, and it was hot as the dickens in Fayetteville. Still, when we drove the car past the sorority houses to impress the ladies, we rolled up the windows and pretended like cool air was blowing, even though we were sweating like a pair of hogs. We drove it so fast and hard that we threw a rod through the motor, so we took it back to the guy we bought it from. Hawg threatened to whip him if he didn't give us our money back, so he did. We owned that car for two days.

Of course, we found other pursuits in that college town on warm spring days and nights. On one of them in particular, Hawg and I and our fetching dates were enjoying ourselves and our alcohol immensely as we cruised around town in the Olds. We finally landed at a Mexican restaurant where our horseplay offended the manager before we'd even gotten a table. When he asked us to settle down, Hawg and I took offense at his tone. We began throwing beer pitchers at him. At that point the manager called out the law, so we decided to take our business to another establishment. We got only a few blocks before two police officers in a squad car pulled us over with red lights flashing. Since I was behind the wheel, the cops gave me a field sobriety test. It wasn't Russian history—I flunked it. They hauled us all off to jail before I hurt myself trying to walk a straight line and booked me for drunk driving. Yet they expected me to make a sober decision on who should drive my car home. Naturally, I chose Hawg.

"Oh, no. He's as drunk as you," the lawman said.

Running out of options, I nominated my curvaceous companion out of Newport, Arkansas, Sissy Hurley. The cops were more than happy to hand her the keys and to be rid of Hawg and his date, too.

I was escorted to a cell, where I found a sympathetic cellmate, a Razorback fan, who'd planned ahead for his own incarceration, bringing along a fried rabbit in a brown paper bag. He was happy to share the meal in exchange for some football stories. I was just chowing down on my lucky rabbit's foot (tasted like chicken) when there came a loud crash from the street outside. I stood on tiptoe to look out the barred window, which offered a view of my beloved Oldsmobile freshly wrapped around a telephone pole. The cops apparently were so saddened by the sight of my wrecked car that they set me free, but only after the last bar had closed so that I wouldn't try to drown my sorrows.

CAREER ADJUSTMENT

It was the last I saw of Sissy, though I never bore her a grudge. The Olds recovered. Unfortunately, my broken arm wasn't such an easy fix. Even after the cast came off, I realized that I couldn't rotate it normally. Nor could I cock my wrist. An offensive receiver needs to have full mobility of his arms and hands. I tested it before I got to camp, and I was not able to make catches that I'd easily made before.

Once I got to camp, it was worse. Frustrated and distraught, I told Coach Parker that I was thinking about quitting. He wasn't sympathetic. He said he couldn't count on a quitter, so I'd better either go ahead and quit or make a major attitude adjustment. I responded well to that sort of challenge. But there wasn't much I could do about my limited range of motion in my hand and arm.

Later that summer, we headed to Chicago to play in the annual exhibition opener, the 1953 College All-Star Game at Soldier Field, a benefit event that pitted the NFL champions against a team of college all-stars from the previous season. I liked Chicago, and I soon discovered that Chicago liked me, too. Unfortunately, it was the Chicago Cardinals who liked me. That week as we practiced, they negotiated a deal with the Lions that brought me to the Windy City as a kicker, defensive end, and occasional tight end.

As much as I enjoyed the city of Chicago, this was not a good deal for me. The Lions were one of the elite teams in the NFL. The Cardinals had just had their third consecutive losing season; even worse, as an organization they were decidedly low-rent. The Bears were Chicago's football team. The Cardinals were like a minor league outfit, and they treated their players accordingly. We played and practiced at Comiskey Field on the south side. It wasn't far from the Chicago stockyards, and to this day I can't smell cow manure without thinking of my time there. That awful odor permeated the entire organization.

The Cardinals were owned by the Bidwell family, the same clan that owns the Arizona incarnation of the Cardinals today. It was a struggling organization back then, even though Charlie Bidwell, who was involved in horse tracks, was one of the founding fathers of the NFL. The Bidwells had a printing business and horse tracks in Chicago. I don't know how they ran those businesses, but their football organization was a poor cousin to the Monsters of the Midway, who ruled at Soldier Field. The Cards enjoyed a brief run, winning the NFL Championship back in 1947, before losing the title game the next year. But the team had been in steady decline since, and had clearly become the Second City's NFL stepchild.

BOMBED OUT

When I arrived at Comiskey for my locker assignment, I walked through the training room and was surprised to see one of the Cardinals linemen sitting in the hot tub, reading the *Racing News* and smoking a cigar, with a bottle of whiskey next to him. I remember thinking, *Good God. That's not how it's supposed to be.* The atmosphere was very different than in Detroit, and while this guy seemed to be more relaxed, I wasn't impressed with what it said about the team's focus and desire.

The first day of practice was not any more encouraging. The practice facilities were at the University of Chicago, which had discontinued its own football program in 1939. The bleachers appeared to be covered with some kind of tar paper, and there were these odd little smokestacks sticking up everywhere in the stands. Finally I asked one of my teammates about them, and he told me they were the remnants from the first nuclear chain reactor built by the University of Chicago's Enrico Fermi. It was only appropriate that the Cardinals practiced atop the site of the birthplace of the world's biggest bomb.

The Cardinals organization was just an oddball outfit. We had some talent, but we struggled under the new head coach, Joe Stydahar. He was the only guy I've ever known to drink whiskey, smoke a cigar, and chew tobacco—all at the same time. He was an intense, driven man, and losing a game was like lighting a fuse for him. He'd had an 18–8 record with his previous team, the Los Angeles Rams; when he moved to Chicago, it was apparent he had neglected to pack whatever had worked for him in L.A.

I was anxious to play again after missing most of my rookie season in Detroit, and the Cardinals were happy to oblige me. I played almost every down on both defense and offense (the lost mobility in my arm did not appear to matter to my new coaches), not to mention special teams, and I did the kicking, too. Despite my heroic efforts, we lost our first seven games, including a thirty-nine point drubbing by Philadelphia, where I played for the first time against rookie defensive back Tom Brookshier. He had a hard head and he knew how to use it, as I would learn many years later.

BAD NEWS BEARS

We tied the Rams at home before taking another beating from Brookshier and the Eagles. I counted once to be sure we had the required number of players; often it didn't seem like it. Our offense had a large hole because our star running back, Ollie Matson, an Olympic track star, was doing his scrambling for the U.S. Army to fulfill a military commitment.

It wasn't hard to get a headcount of our fans, either. We played in a stadium with forty thousand seats, only about one-third of them filled for most games. Chicago's south siders had not really embraced us. Mostly they enjoyed calling us names related to things found in the stockyards. It was colorful, but not pretty.

My teammates got along well, probably as a survival thing since we were usually under assault by our opponents, our fans, and our coaches. We partied together and commiserated about the crappy Cardinal organization, its equipment, its practice facilities, and its coaching staff. The owners had the money, they just weren't sharing it with the team. The team's founder, Charlie Bidwell, had died a number of years before, and his widow, Violet, was not all that interested in the team she'd inherited.

We were a neglected team, but we entertained each other. During the season, the players roomed at the Piccadilly Hotel on the south side of Chicago near Comiskey. The accommodations were by no means luxurious, but we really didn't care. We'd go downtown to the Chicago Loop for dinner once a week, and on Monday nights we'd descend upon the Caribbean Room in the Hyde Park Hotel for the weekly amateur singing contest. Our secret weapon was the offensive captain, Jack Jennings, the big tackle from Ohio State. He'd belt out "Ballin' the Jack" and win every time because the judges were afraid we'd tear the place apart if our man didn't take the prize. The house piano player, the lovely Mary Jo Kinkade, was also on our team because we'd always give her a cut of the $25 prize money. Then we'd drink up the rest, drowning our football sorrows.

We staggered to an awful 0-10-1 record, going into the last game of the year against our cross-town rival, the Bears. The mood of our coach, like our record, was in the dumps. For the last game, he resorted to threats: "If you don't beat the Bears this week, none of you will get your last check. None of you!"

It was not exactly a classic inspirational speech, like Knute Rockne's "Win one for the Gipper," but the prospect of no pay and a winless season did the trick. Fortunately, the Bears were having a mediocre season, too, so they weren't exactly the Monsters of the Midway at that point. We beat them 24–17, saving us from a winless season and blank paychecks. Still, we finished with the worst record in the league: second to last in both offense and defense.

It was remarkable that we managed to be so bad with four Pro Bowl players, including my roommate, the All-American running back from the University of California, Johnny Olszewski. We also had University of Georgia All-American halfback/quarterback Charley Trippi and defensive back Don Paul. Don "Stoney" Stonesifer was a standout receiver, as was Gern Nagler. I'd done my part to help our sputtering offense. I'd made all twenty-three extra-point conversions, but just nine field goals.

FARM LEAGUE

It had been a long, cold season. I cleared out my locker and headed south to Lake City as soon as it ended. I was able to land a job as a substitute teacher for the rest of the school year, and I used my NFL earnings to bankroll a business with P. A. Browning, the principal at the junior high where I was teaching. P. A. was also a produce farmer, so he convinced me to join him in expanding his operation. Under his guidance, I became a genuine sodbuster. We bought a hundred acres near Lake City and another hundred just outside Ocala, to the south. We planted watermelon, bell peppers, tomatoes, and squash. It was more work than I'd ever done in my life, laboring in the fields baked by the Florida sun. But in our first year we had ideal growing conditions and the market was prime. We each ended up with $50,000 in profits. My cut was nearly ten times my NFL salary.

It looked like my future was in farming. I actually stayed with it for about five years, helping P. A. produce watermelon, tomatoes, squash, bell peppers, and anything else we could pull out of the ground. We kept putting our earnings back into the soil, eventually buying another two hundred acres in parcels near Apopka and Lake Okeechobee.

The gritty work of farming gave me a new appreciation for football, and the watermelon operation, in particular, bulked me up like never before. My hands and arms grew stronger from catching, carrying, and packing our huge Florida watermelons. And I became an expert at packing them into semitrailers so that they didn't get smashed en route from our farm fields to markets in New York City. The temperature would hit 140 degrees in those trailers, so I had to rehydrate by drinking a case of beer a day. Still, I went back to training camp in the best shape of my life.

RIDING THE NIGHT TRAIN

We had hoped for a better season in 1954, mostly because our star running back, Ollie Matson, was returning from his year of military service. The Cardinals also had drafted my old Arkansas teammate, quarterback Lamar McHan, and we'd picked up a terrific diamond in the rough, cornerback Richard "Night Train" Lane, in a trade with the Los Angeles Rams.

Night Train was an amazing physical specimen who'd risen to stardom and folk hero status from a hardscrabble life. Abandoned in a dumpster as an infant, he was raised in poverty by the woman who found him. He'd played football at a junior college and never got any attention from bigger schools or the pros, so after serving in the military and reaching the rank of lieutenant colonel, he went to work in an aircraft factory.

After months of grueling work wrestling with sheets of metal, he gave football one last try. He talked his way into a tryout with the Rams. The coaches were impressed by his power, speed, and attitude. He signed a $5,000 contract, and in his first season set a pass-interception record that's yet to be broken, picking off fourteen in the twelve-game season. At six foot two and 210 pounds, Night Train had deceptive speed and a vicious tackling style, known as the "Night Train Necktie," that terrified his opponents and resulted in a rule that banned tacklers from "clotheslining" anyone by hitting them above the shoulders.

I never saw Night Train lose a wind sprint in practice. He even beat Matson, the former Olympic sprinter. In fact, Night Train sometimes ran sprints in drills with his hands in his pocket—and he still whipped us all. The one knock on this great athlete was that he gambled too much on defense. Often, he'd tell the safety, "Cover me deep, because I'm goin' for the interception." Of course, the safety had his own responsibilities to worry about, so Night Train's freelancing sometimes resulted in a big play for the other team. Still, he picked off ten passes in his first year with the Cardinals and led the league in interceptions, so he earned his $5,000 contract.

UNCOOL COACH

Night Train, Matson, and McHan were great players, but they weren't enough to carry us to a winning season. We started the 1954 season losing five straight. Our coach responded by losing his cool, if not his mind. Stydahar issued a decree prohibiting sex before games. You can imagine how that went over. I fully expected a team baby boom to result. Our one-of-a-kind coach also took to writing insults on our paychecks, but that wasn't nearly as exciting as the one payday when he threw our checks up in the air and said, "Fight for them, you gutless suckers."

If he intended these insults to motivate us to greater achievements on the field, it didn't. My highlight film was a very short feature, if not a cartoon, that year. I kicked and played defense, but it wasn't pretty for any of us. We finished the year 2-10. Our record did motivate the team owners to fire Stydahar, ending his career as an NFL coach. His combined Cardinals record: 3-20-1.

PLANTING ROOTS

I returned to Lake City once again, where the growing season was also the pits. Once again we worked until our fingers bled and our backs ached, but this time the weather didn't cooperate. There were frosts in portions of Florida that year, and we always seemed to have a patch in the path of the cold fronts. We didn't make a nickel on watermelon that second year, after hauling in $50,000 each in my rookie season as a Florida truck farmer. Fortunately we'd planted about sixty acres in green peppers, squash, and green beans, so we did make about $10,000 each.

Between football and farming and my off-season teaching job in Lake City, I was pulling in about $18,000 annually and feeling like a grown-up for the first time in my life. Closing in on twenty-five years old, I had also settled down into the most serious relationship of my active but unstable social life. I started dating Kathy Jacobs when I returned to Lake City after the 1954–55 season in Chicago. She was a local girl, but I was four years older, so I'd never known her when I was in high school. By the time I met her, she was finishing her senior year in college. A dark-haired Southern belle, she was the soft-spoken, deeply religious daughter of a retired army colonel. Her father had done well raising Tennessee Walking horses in Tennessee until the Depression wiped out his business. He'd retired after that and moved his family to Lake City.

Kathy wasn't much of a sports fan, but most people weren't much impressed with professional football players back then. (It was considered a cut above a blue-collar job and not a glamorous career, at least not in Lake City.) She was very grounded, unlike most of the college girls I'd dated. I liked that, given the unsettled, transient nature of my life to that point. Nearly all of my Lake City buddies were married and starting families. Our friends considered us the nearly "perfect couple," our only flaw being that we hadn't walked down the aisle yet. We were enjoying just being a couple. We even spent one summer working together at a Girl Scout camp. She was a counselor and I was a lifeguard, and we became closer than ever before.

The Cardinals were such a bad organization that I was already looking forward to life after football. I'd hoped to settle down in Lake City, where I felt at home with so many friends and family. My grandmother had passed away, but my cousin Mike and his parents were still there. That was what Kathy wanted, too, so it seemed destined.

I was in no rush, though. Even when we started talking about getting married just a few months into our relationship, I was thinking I'd play one more year of pro football and then we'd tie the knot. But her father had his own ideas about the timetable. He was a gruff but wonderful old guy. When he heard that we were talking marriage, his military training kicked in. He wanted a plan of attack and a course of action. And, of course, he was in command.

"I understand you want to marry my daughter," he said. "Do you have any money?"

I told him of my combined earnings, which seemed pretty impressive to me at the time.

"When do you want to do it?" he said.

"I want to play one more year of pro football and then quit to come back here and farm and teach," I said.

"No, I think if you're going to do this, let's get it done," my future father-in-law said.

And so, Kathy and I were married in July of 1955. Oddly enough, my arms-length father chose to come a bit closer just before the wedding to offer the only two pieces of advice I can remember him giving me. It was just something he threw at me out of the blue, and he didn't bother to elaborate.

"I've met very few honest men in my life. There aren't many of them from what I've seen. I hope you turn out to be one—an honest man."

The second bit of sage wisdom was less high-minded: "Don't let women screw up your life."

NEW SEASON KICKOFF

My father's second piece of advice probably wasn't the most fitting thought to have in mind at the start of a marriage. Still, I returned to Chicago for a new football season with Kathy at my side. We took our own apartment at the Piccadilly Hotel. It wasn't the honeymoon suite, but it was affordable and close to Comiskey Park.

Ray Richards made his pro coaching debut for the Cardinals that season. Under him, we made some progress, winning four, losing seven, and tying one. That was more wins than we'd had the previous two seasons combined. I played mostly defensive end, had eight field goals and twenty-three extra points, and scored my first—and only—NFL touchdown.

Jim Finks, who later became general manager of the Bears and the New Orleans Saints, was Pittsburgh's quarterback that day. I was playing defensive end, and I could sense from Pittsburgh's blocking scheme that they were trying to slip a guy past me for a screen pass. So instead of rushing the passer, I backed off at the last second while Finks was rushed hard. Sure enough, he tried to dump a screen pass over me. I backpedaled like a guilty politician, nearly losing my balance. But it was another lucky day for me. The football hit me in the helmet, bounced straight up in the air, and then fell into my outstretched arms.

Instinct kicked in, and I scrambled across the goal line for a score from twenty-six yards out. It was all skill, all the way, except for the part where it bounced off my helmet and into my arms. My teammates weren't overly impressed. Mostly they teased me about the fact that someone had been gaining on me, and that if the field were any longer I might never have made it. But I did!

I managed to score a few more points in my career, but that was the only time I carried the ball across the goal line. In those days, field goals were not a common offensive weapon. Kickers were not given the opportunity to become consistent. When we were called onto the field it was usually as a last resort or an afterthought. It's a shame; I could have kicked a lot more field goals if I'd been given the chance, but even I never envisioned kickers playing the major roles they do today.

There were some guys who hinted of things to come. One of them was Lou "The Toe" Groza, who was routinely winning games for Cleveland with his kicking foot.

Unlike today's soccer-style kicking, which is more like a golf swing, kickers in my day were straightaway kickers who had to connect with the ball perfectly. It was a more strenuous form of kicking, and our legs tired easily. We couldn't practice all that much for fear of wearing our legs out or developing bad habits.

There was also the fact that nobody wanted to hold for me, and they didn't have anybody to shag balls. So everything I kicked, I had to chase down if I wanted to kick again. As a result, I didn't get more than twenty-five or thirty kicks each practice. If I did find someone to hold for me, it was only because they were under threat of losing their jobs. It was one of the most undesirable, all-guts-no-glory duties next to snapping the ball for field goals or extra points. I had an ever-changing series of guys to hold the ball for me, and it was tough to get in a groove with so many different styles to deal with.

Holding the ball is still considered one of the worst jobs in pro football. If something goes wrong, it's always the holder's fault; if it goes right, nobody even remembers who was holding the ball. It's also an awkward and difficult task. You've got to crouch on the ground in a defensive position, catch the ball, spin it so that the laces are away from the kicker, and then hope that he doesn't punt your fingers into the stands. The good centers will know how many times the ball is going to spin to get it to the holder with the laces away. Still, the holder has a lot going on, and while he's trying to focus, a bunch of very large, determined men are running at him with malevolent intentions. In late 1955, one of my holders, defensive back Tom Keane, got slammed while he was holding for me; he never played the game again.

Like I said, it was a dirty job, and it didn't make kickers any more popular when their holders were regarded as sacrificial lambs.

We sputtered to the finish line in that 1955 season, losing four of our last five games, finishing 4-7-1. I did manage to kick some field goals and gain some respect around the league as a guy who could put points on the board, if his team could get close enough to the end zone.

It was the Cardinals' sixth consecutive losing season. Football fans packed the stands in Chicago, but not at Comiskey Park. They were a few miles up the road at Wrigley Field, where the Bears were back in contention.

COACH SUMMERALL

When Kathy and I returned to Lake City for the off-season, I fulfilled a promise I'd made to her father, the Colonel. When he granted me permission to marry her, one of his conditions was that she would finish her degree at Florida State University. So we headed to Tallahassee for the spring semester.

FSU had been an all-girls' school when I was in college, but they'd opened the doors to the boys by then. They'd even fielded a football team, and I wrangled an assistant coaching job to keep myself busy. I'd often thought I might want to try coaching some day, so this was my chance to see if I was any good at it. Tom Nugent was the head coach, and he put me in charge of the kickers and the offensive ends that spring. Just to make sure I had enough to do, they also gave me a class to teach—bowling. But there was no bowling alley on campus, and no equipment either, so mostly I taught bowling theory while my class tried to stay awake in the stands of the football stadium.

I had a lot of fun and made some long-term friends even if I didn't inspire anyone with my coaching—either in football or bowling. The FSU Seminoles had some colorful young players that year. Two of the wildest were roommates: Lee Corso, a running back who became a college coach and sportscaster, and his bunkmate, defensive back Buddy Reynolds, later known as Burt. For an actor, he wasn't a bad football player, but his best moves were in the sororities and girls' dormitories. Buddy was the darling of the cheerleaders even before he was a movie star.

Years later, he showed up in the booth during a Sun Bowl broadcast, and we reminisced about that spring training season in Tallahassee. As we spoke there in the open booth, grown women pelted us with their under-garments and room keys. For a brief moment, I thought I was the object of their affections, but they quickly put me on notice that Buddy's hairy-chested charms had only grown during his "Burt" years.

BACK TO WORK

As much fun as I had in Tallahassee, I had to go back to work for the 1956 season with the Cardinals. It wasn't as dreary as I had feared it would be. We got off to a good start, with four straight wins, including road blowouts at Washington and Philadelphia. We put in the "split T" formation; nobody had ever seen it, and the teams couldn't adjust to it. McHan, Matson, and Night Train were in their prime, as was cornerback Lindon Crow, who had eleven interceptions that year. We contended for the division title most of the year, then had a stretch in late season where we dropped four out of five games and—you guessed it—slowly faded out of contention.

We finished the season 7-5, a game and a half behind the New York Giants. Even though it was the Cardinals' first winning season since 1949, I was extremely frustrated at our poor finish. We just couldn't close the deal. We lost four out of our five losing games that year by a narrow margin—a touchdown or less. I feared we'd blown our one shot at the championship. There were no Wild Card teams in postseason back then, just one championship game between winners of the East and West Divisions. So we all went home and tried to earn enough money in the off-season to support our football habits.

SQUASHED

If the glories of professional football were fading, the shine was definitely wearing off my sideline as a Florida farmer. Kathy was a gracious Southern belle, but she was not a farmer's daughter, and the role of farmer's wife wasn't her natural cup of tea, either.

"I don't ever want to see another squash," she said one day in exasperation.

I couldn't blame her. We'd had one very good year that had triggered visions of agricultural grandeur, then a couple of not-so-good years brought me back down to earth. There are a lot of things you can do to make a football team better, but farmers have no control over the most important factor in their livelihoods: the weather.

My plans for the future were looking a little shaky on both the football and the farming fronts as I returned to Chicago for the 1957 season. As a team, it turned out to be our worst season, though I managed to have some good times with an old buddy from my Razorback days. Defensive backend Floyd Sagely came over to the Cardinals in a trade from the San Francisco 49ers. We teamed up on and off the field, and raised more than a few toasts to our college days. It was a good thing we'd had those glory days, because there wasn't much to toast about our shared season with the Cardinals. We did open with a road win against Floyd's old club, then we went to 2–2 before dropping six games in a row—four at home.

BEAT UP

That was it. We finished the season with a lopsided home loss to Pittsburgh, giving us a 3–9 record. I could hear the hogs at home calling me. Floyd was even more frustrated. He was playing safety to Night Train's gambling man. It put Floyd in a no-win situation. If Night Train gambled and won, he was a hero. If he gambled and lost, Floyd looked foolish.

The Chicago newspapers were all over us, and rightfully so. There were rumblings about moving the team to Minneapolis or St. Louis or Buffalo, cities that were hungry—starving, apparently—for a pro football franchise. We even played a game in Buffalo to test the waters there. Meanwhile, my old team the Lions was on its way to winning three out of four championship games they played in the 1950s.

For the first time since I started playing football, I was giving serious thought to giving it up. The money was okay, but I still had to work in the off-season to stay ahead. I loved the game, but these losing seasons were getting to me. One of the bright spots of the year had been reuniting with my old friend Sagely. But at the end of the year he said he was hanging up his spikes. He'd had enough. I told him I'd considered it, but I thought I might stick around another year or so. I tried to talk him into doing the same, but his mind was made up.

One reason I did not quit was the arrival of an impressive new coach hired by the Cardinals. Frank "Pop" Ivy had been a receiver on the Cardinals' lone championship team in 1947. As a young assistant coach at the University of Oklahoma, he helped the Sooners to an undefeated national championship season in 1950, and in his rookie year as a head coach in the Canadian Football League in 1954, he led the Edmonton Eskimos to the first of three consecutive Grey Cup Championships.

I had a long talk with "Pop"—so named because of his premature baldness—soon after he got to the Cardinals job. He was known as an innovative offensive coach, so I was intrigued about what my role would be. When I asked, he said, "Pat, you're one of our building blocks, one of the keys to our success. You're going to play both ways and be our kicker. We're counting on you."

I went back home to Florida encouraged by the words of praise from the new guy in charge. Then, just prior to the opening of training camp for the 1958 season, I read in the Jacksonville newspaper that I had been traded. My new coach had been feeding me a line of bull. Cornerback Linden Crow and I were going to the New York Giants for Bobby Joe Conrad and Dick Nolan.

No matter how may times you've been through it, any pro athlete will tell you that being traded is one of the worst feelings in the world. But at least it would be a new beginning. The Cards had finished in the cellar in 1957, while the Giants contended for the NFL East crown in 1957 after winning the NFL Championship the year before. Moving from Lake City to New York City would be a huge change, but it was nothing like moving from the Cardinals to the Giants.

CHAPTER FOUR

GIANT STEP UP

THE GIANTS' TRAINING CAMP WAS A LONG WAY FROM THE NEON LIGHTS of Broadway and Times Square. It was more like the land time forgot. We were in Salem, Oregon, about three thousand miles away from the distractions of the big city. In those days, teams often set up camp in faraway places. The bad teams did it so their fans couldn't figure out ahead of time how bad they were going to be. The good teams didn't want the competition to know what was in store. And the Giants were about the best going in those days.

In my first few hours there, I thought it was being deep in the backwoods of the Northwest that made everything seem so strange at this camp, but I soon figured out it was the unfamiliar efficiency that was throwing me off. It hit me that I was in a whole new ballgame at the first team meeting. I took a seat next to the Giants backup quarterback, Don Heinrich, and felt like I was joining a party in progress. The players were teasing each other, telling jokes, and laughing.

The Cardinals team meetings had often seemed like wakes, and not even Irish wakes. This was happy hour without the booze. An assistant coach was attempting to take roll call over the din, but with little success. Suddenly, another assistant coach—a short, no-neck bull of a guy with wiry black hair and eyeglasses as thick as glass block—appeared at the front of the room. He cleared his throat. And there was absolute silence. It happened so fast I actually thought my hearing had given out.

I turned to Heinrich and whispered, "Who is that?"

"Lombardi," he said.

Vince Lombardi was the Giants' offensive coach, but he seemed more like their General Patton. He spoke with complete authority, and his record as a coach backed it up. He'd come to the Giants in 1954 after their miserable 3–9 season. They'd had a winning season ever since, capped by an NFL Championship.

Lombardi wasn't the only reason this was a great organization. They also had an assistant defensive coach by the name of Tom Landry, an entirely different sort of person than Lombardi, but this wiry, whip-smart guy was another football mastermind headed for legendary status.

The Giants were obviously blessed in the coaching department; I soon discovered that the move had other perks as well. From the uniforms and helmets, to the towels and the soap in the locker room shower, it was like moving from the No-Tell Motel to the Ritz Carlton. The organization's investment in quality was reflected in the team they put on the field. The Giants carried themselves with the confidence of champions, and that in itself gave them an advantage over most opponents.

TRIMMED-BACK DUTY

I was familiar with the Giants' players from being thumped by them in recent years, but I was more well-acquainted with their head coach, Jim Lee Howell, who had played at the University of Arkansas and later with the Giants. Coach Howell had spent some time as an administrator at Razorback Hall between his playing and coaching days, where I'd gotten to know and like him.

I called him after I learned of my trade to see what he had in mind for me. "You're going to be the kicker, and we want you to play both ways—not so much as a regular, but as a backup," he said.

That was welcome news after so many years of playing practically every play of every game; I was ready for a little down time between downs. The Giants' kicker from the previous year, Ben Agajanian, had been in the league since 1945. He was a kicking specialist, which limited the flexibility of a team with the tight thirty-three man roster.

Agajanian also had a few quirks that made him expendable. He had a garbage business with his brother in California, and Ben cut hair on the side in training camp—not too well—and in his neighborhood in the off-season. The Giants laid down the law after the 1957 season, so the team barber quit, setting up their trade for me. I didn't mind stepping in as kicker, but I refused to curl and dye anybody's hair.

Still, I fit in quickly with the jovial Giants crew. The team talent didn't end with the coaching staff. Their dream roster included former Southern Methodist University and all-world star Kyle Rote, halfback Alex Webster, halfback and wide receiver Frank Gifford, linebacker Sam Huff, quarterback Charlie Conerly, defensive end Andy Robustelli, defensive back Emlen Tunnell, defensive tackle and defensive end Roosevelt "Rosey" Grier, and another big "Rosey," tackle Roosevelt Brown. Don Chandler was our punter, and Don Maynard, a wide receiver, was a Giants rookie in 1958.

Aside from all their athletic gifts, this was a bunch of bright and charismatic guys. Many of them went on to more fortune or fame after they stopped playing football. Rote and Gifford became noted broadcasters, along with one other guy on the team whose name I can't recall.

ALL-STAR COACHING

Training camp was a revelation. Lombardi had forgotten more than most other coaches knew. He had played college ball at Fordham, and later served as an assistant coach at West Point under Earl "Colonel Red" Blaik, widely considered the best college coach in the country. Blaik taught Lombardi to focus on fundamentals, strive for perfect execution, and conduct himself like a gentleman. Lombardi had all that and more. He was also the greatest teacher I'd ever encountered, on or off the field. No detail was too small for him to master and then drill into us.

He knew exactly how long a pulling right guard's first step had to be if he was going to clear the quarterback's feet. He taught things over and over until they became instinct. Lombardi was such a dynamic leader that no one questioned him. That alone saved hours of time. We simply did our jobs as we were told. The really impressive thing was that he listened just as well as he talked. And if he didn't have a specific answer for some oddball question, you could count on Lombardi to go to his favorite tip: "When all else fails, just react like a football player," he'd say.

Then again, if you made a good suggestion, Lomabardi embraced it and put it in the playbook. If you told him something wasn't working, he wasn't afraid to acknowledge that, too. In my first training camp he was trying to teach us an offensive scheme West Point ran called "the Belly Series." In it, the quarterback got the snap, then without releasing the ball would hold it against the belly of the in-motion fullback, while turning toward the line to watch the reaction of the defense. If the defense started to follow the fullback, the quarterback would retract the ball and pitch it out to the halfback, much like the option or "split T" formation.

Quarterbacks didn't like the series because they saw the potential for opposing linemen to knock the crap out of them. We also had a tough time making it work in practice. Our monster fullback, Mel Triplett, had taken a few too many hits to his helmet. He fumbled a couple of the "belly" handoffs, frustrating Lombardi. The coach grabbed the ball and said, "Here, I'll show you how to run it." Lombardi took the snap, brought the ball back, and put it in Triplett's belly. But Mel got confused and not only ran over Lombardi, he also stepped on his throat, almost collapsing his windpipe.

Lombardi got up, dusted himself off, and, once he could breath again, even laughed about it. But that was the end of "the Belly Series."

"DEACON" LANDRY

Our defensive coach, Tom Landry, who played for the Giants from 1950 to 1955, was not into the Socratic method of teaching football. He was more of a church deacon giving orders from the pulpit. It was, "Do this and that, and we'll win." Amen. Pass the collection plate. He didn't believe in taking suggestions from the congregation.

In my Cardinal days, I'd played against Landry a few times since he had been a defensive back. He could deliver a hard lick, so you knew he was tough to the core. But as a coach, he seemed emotionless, always very cool and focused. He never raised his voice in anger, and he never offered praise, either. Later, when he was head coach of the Dallas Cowboys, I was surprised to hear Bob Lilly get what seemed like the highest praise I'd ever heard from Landry. "I've had good players in my coaching career, both with Giants and Cowboys," Landry said. "But there's only one Bob Lilly."

Still, Landry was a master strategist on defense. He built a customized 4-3 defense around Huff, creating a middle linebacker position. With Huff, a human pit bull, in that assassin's role, Landry hoped to stop a couple of legendary runners in the league: Jim Brown of Cleveland and Green Bay's Jim Taylor. Later in his coaching career, Landry was a widely copied innovator; one of his most notable contributions was the "Flex" defense, which was ironic, given his inflexibility as a coach.

With Landry, you never knew how you were doing. If you made a good play, he'd nod. That constituted high praise. Yet the guy knew football. He served as kicking coach, too, and he was an excellent one. He had been a good punter at the University of Texas, and in the NFL he averaged more than forty yards a punt with the Giants. Landry had placekicking down, too. He watched me practice and quickly spotted my tendencies, both good and bad. He coached me to "groove" a kicking style much like golfers try to do with their golf swings. The idea is to find a style that works and do it that way every time. This produced a more relaxed and smooth kicking style, which delivered more power.

His coaching tips definitely made a difference. With the Cardinals, I made about 50 percent of my field goal attempts. I improved a great deal on that with the Giants, thanks to Landry's coaching and also to my exceptional holder, Charlie Conerly. Known at Ole Miss as "All-American Chunkin' Charlie," he'd played one year before taking a four-year break to serve in the U.S. Marines. Then he came back and played out the rest of his college eligibility, setting three NCAA records for passing yardage. Charlie was about thirty-seven years old by the time we teamed up. He was a tough ol' boy, and he didn't mess around. If Charlie thought you were a bad kicker, he wouldn't go out on the field with you. Lucky for me, we worked well together. He had great hands, and he had holding down to a blue-collar art form. It also helped that Charlie wasn't worried about someone creaming him when he was in a vulnerable position holding for me. He looked like he could chew a football to shreds. We made such a good team on the field we eventually roomed together when we were on the road for games. I made it a point to keep Charlie on my side.

YANKEE HOME

Training camp ended, and we headed east to the Big Apple from the forests of the Northwest for the 1958 season. Once again, culture shock set in. It wasn't just the bright lights, the crazy traffic, and the media pack. I was a professional athlete, but I was still a starstruck sports fan, too. And for the first few weeks as the baseball and football seasons overlapped, we shared a locker room at Yankee Stadium with the New York Yankees. Imagine my shock, then, when I went to my assigned locker and found the name "Mickey Mantle" on it.

That same name was in the sports headlines every day. Mickey was having a great season. He had forty home runs and an incredible batting average. The Yanks were on their way to another World Series appearance. I had met Mickey though his twin brothers when I briefly played minor-league ball with them in the St. Louis Cardinals' organization. He tended to keep people at arm's length because so many strangers wanted a piece of him, but we grew to be close buddies from seeing so much of each other in the locker room.

Until the Giants finished their extended season, we were a traveling team. We took a bus from the stadium to our temporary practice fields at nearby Fordham University. It was home turf for Lombardi. He'd played there as a member of the famed "Seven Blocks of Granite" defensive line. He'd also graduated with honors in business.

We were gypsies off the field, too. The Giants players and their families stayed at the Concourse Plaza on 161st Street, which was less than three blocks from Yankee Stadium; not exactly a luxurious place to lodge. A lot of the Yankee players—including Mickey—lived in apartments in that same general area of the Bronx, so we ran into them in the local bars and restaurants. It was one heck of a neighborhood, and we had some hellacious block parties. Conerly had a friend at a health club, and we'd play basketball together when we were off on Mondays, get massages, and then go out to watch the Monday night fights at St. Francis Arena in Brooklyn. It was a relaxing boys' night out, but I didn't always get a warm reception when I got home to Kathy. She resented being left alone with our baby daughter, Susie, particularly when I came home smelling like a brewery after midnight.

GAME TIME

We did manage to find time to play some good football, too. I tried not to feel too cocky about our first win over my old tattered-and-torn Cardinals team, whipping them 37–7. Maybe that win came too easy, because we lost the next two out of three games.

I knew once our sleeping Giants awakened, we'd kick some tail, and we did. We won the next three, thanks to our marquee players. Kyle Rote averaged twenty yards a catch on creaking knees. Frank Gifford had four yards a carry, and Don Chandler was averaging forty-four yards per punt. We capped the win streak with a rough and tumble 24–21 win over a very talented Baltimore Colts team. It was an especially sweet win because it came on the strength of a field goal by the new guy—me.

Still, when it came to kicking field goals in Yankee Stadium, there was no home field advantage. It was a plain awful place to kick. It was Yankee Stadium, not Giant Stadium. The groundskeeper never let us forget it. We weren't allowed to use the right field area because they didn't want us to tear up Mickey's turf. So our football playing field was pushed over into the dirt infield. It made for some very unpredictable kicking surfaces, and it was not a fun place to get tackled, either.

By season's end, we were playing on dirt and mud that the groundskeepers lamely tried to disguise by painting it green. Nobody was fooled, and the laundry bill was sky-high since the paint wore off on our jerseys, pants, and helmets.

I was worse for the wear, too. I had been in the league for seven years, and the dirt field only aggravated my aches and pains. In my younger days, it only took me a day or two to recover from a game. Now it was Wednesday or Thursday before I could walk and run like a normal human being.

We were 8–3 going into our last regular-season game. We had to beat the 9–2 Cleveland Browns at Yankee Stadium to tie for the NFL East title. A win would force a playoff game against the same Cleveland team the next week to determine who would move onto the title game against the Colts in the West. Baltimore already had iced their division championship. Back then the Browns–Giants rivalry was considered the fiercest in the NFL, but we won an epic battle on their turf, 21–17, in early November. Cleveland was led by the freight train masquerading as running back Jim Brown. With legs like bridge beams, he was next to unstoppable for most of the season, scoring seventeen touchdowns and gaining more than fifteen hundred yards on almost six yards a carry.

MAN AMONG WEENIES

Tackling Jim Brown was the toughest task in football. He was a hulk of a man who made the rest of us look like weenies. To stop most ball carriers, you'd hit and wrap around them, then hang on until your sheer weight made them collapse. That didn't happen with Brown. He'd just keep running while you and the rest of your team dragged behind like so many tin cans on a string. He was stronger, faster, and bigger than any other back in the league. And it got so guys hated to see him coming at them because as he gained confidence, he got better and better and tougher and tougher.

Once Brown established his dominance in the league, he liked to circle his opponents as they warmed up before our games, like a lion picking out the weak and the slow in the herd. He knew how to intimidate people. He was also sneaky. On those momentous occasions when he did get tackled (usually by everyone on the roster), Brown would stay on the ground, acting as though he'd had a rib broken or a leg crushed. He'd always drag himself back to the huddle with a limp. Then, before you knew it, the quarterback was handing him the ball and he was exploding for sixty yards downfield.

The Giants had more success against Brown than most, thanks to Landry's revolutionary 4-3 defense. But it was still tough to contain him and the rest of their offense. We had our hands full because our season depended on beating them three times that season.

Game day arrived cold and blustery at Yankee Stadium in the Bronx. Snow had been falling since early morning. The thought of hitting that frozen field made me wish I was back in my hog pens in Lake City. Then, on the first play from scrimmage, Brown went eighty yards for the score. The weather slowed him down after that. As the game progressed and the elements worsened, neither offense could generate much traction on the increasingly slippery surface. It became a battle in the trenches, with both teams trying to pound out a few yards at a time. Suddenly, the kickers had a major role. Both Cleveland's Lou Groza and I kicked one field goal each to add to each team's single touchdown. It was deadlocked 10–10 late in the game.

CALLED TO KICK

We didn't need a tie. Only a win would take us into the playoffs. We managed to string together a nice drive toward the end of the game, and were on the twenty-four yard line on fourth down. I ran out on to the field for what could be a game-winning field goal, but in the swirling wind, I missed wide from thirty-one yards out. I felt like I'd let my new team down in a big way. Heads were hanging when I got to the sidelines. But this was a classy team with classy guys. They were winners who didn't give up. Linebacker Cliff Livingston came up to me, slapped me on the back, and said, "We're gonna get you another chance."

I had my doubts. Maybe I was suffering from a Cardinal hangover, but it occurred to me that, even if we got the ball back, it was going to be tough to move it to the goal line in the blizzard that had descended. Our archrivals were looking good for the title game unless we got a break. They played it smart by running the ball and not taking any chances. They obviously were willing to take the tie. But they played a bit too conservatively, and we held them on that first series, forcing them to punt with about two minutes remaining.

Our team managed to get the ball just past midfield. Then Conerly hit sure-handed Alex Webster with a perfect pass in the end zone on third down. We thought we had it won. But Webster dropped it.

Suddenly, all eyes were on me. Our only hope was a field goal, a virtually impossible field goal in the worst conditions imaginable.

The line of scrimmage was rumored to be somewhere around the Browns' forty-five yard line, but we needed a snowplow and an ice pick to find it. Even with the goal posts on the goal line, instead of the end line where they are today, I was looking at one nightmare of an attempt. I'd made a few from that distance, but always in balmy sunshine. I really thought the coaches would decide a field goal was out of reach.

Instead, Jim Lee Howell walked over to me and said, "Okay, field goal."

Stunned, I trotted out to the huddle. I wasn't super confident, and my pal Charlie didn't help things. When I got to the huddle, he looked up and said, "What are you doin' here?"

"They sent me in to kick the field goal."

"You're kiddin'!" Conerly said.

Sorry, Charlie.

KICK OF A LIFETIME

I made the mistake of looking toward the distant goal shrouded in a heavy curtain of falling snow. The wind was howling. My breath was a vapor cloud hovering in front of my face. Lacking ice picks, Charlie and I kicked out a little clearing for my feet. I was disoriented without yard markers to measure the distance. This was the closest thing to a blind kick I'd ever had to attempt. The goal post looked like it had shrunk in the cold. I did a little self-coaching and told myself all I could do was kick the ball as hard as I could and hope that my leg didn't shatter like an icicle dropped off the roof.

It was a good snap and a good hold. As soon as I kicked it, I knew it was going to be far enough, but the ball was on a very unpromising trajectory, knuckleballing like a missile gone awry. Yet, somehow, it stayed on course and cleared the uprights by so much it would have been good from sixty-five yards out!

A mob of teammates hit me like a runaway snowplow. I'm not sure how I ever dug out and got to the sideline, but the first guy to grab me there was Lombardi. I knew he'd argued with his head coach to go for a first down. But I figured he'd be so happy that he'd forget that he'd been overruled and proven wrong. Not Lombardi. There were no congratulations from him. Instead he growled, "You son of a bitch, you know you can't kick it that far!"

There are still bar fights over just how long that kick actually was. Kyle Rote claimed it was from the fifty yard line. Others argue that it was even longer. It went down in the record books as a forty-nine yard field goal. Whatever the distance, it was a glorious moment for me.

Still, we had a game to finish. Cleveland had not surrendered.

After we kicked off, the Browns couldn't do anything with the ball. They ran out of time and we ran off with the game. We had dodged a bullet with my impossible kick. We were headed for a playoff the next week. After the game, the debate about the distance of the field goal continued. Giants co-owner Wellington Mara, then club vice president, called it the most significant play in franchise history. But even he second-guessed the decision to go for it. Coach Howell had gone out on a limb all by himself in calling for me to kick it. To this day, Webster tells me, "If I hadn't dropped that pass, nobody would've ever heard of you!"

The miracle kick had a big psychological impact. The Browns never recovered their cockiness. We whipped them 10–0 in the next playoff game. It wasn't like we'd been putting fans to sleep in the first two games, but the next one—the championship game against the Baltimore Colts—was one for the ages.

A GAME TO REMEMBER

We were at home again, which was a good thing because our butts were dragging. I don't think I had the strength to pack. By nearly every assessment, we were the underdogs. The book on us was that we'd gotten some lucky bounces in our defeat of the Colts earlier in the season. The Colts, coached by Weeb Eubank, had the dynamic duo of quarterback Johnny Unitas and wide receiver Raymond Berry. Unitas was like some mythical beast, an ogre with a golden arm. Berry had always given us fits. They also had a tough running back in Alan "The Horse" Ameche. Let's see, what else? A strong defense, and they were much more rested than we were since they had wrapped up their division early on. While we were fighting off frostbite against the Browns, they were roasting their chestnuts by the open fire.

There were sixty-four thousand fans at the championship game, and not many of them gave us a chance. We didn't exactly change a lot of minds early in the game. Frank Gifford—normally a sure-handed wonder—fumbled twice, and the Colts pranced off for touchdowns. We went into halftime trailing 14–3.

But the Giants were stouthearted men. We came back strong in the second half. Mel Triplett scored on a dive from the one-yard line and then the golden Gifford atoned for the miscues of his first half by pulling in a fifteen-yard touchdown pass from creaking Conerly. That put us up 17–14.

With less than two minutes to play, the Colts put the ball in play from their own fourteen, and Unitas went to work. He hit Lenny Moore for eleven yards, then Berry for twenty-five, sixteen, and twenty-one. It was a berry, berry bad time for us. All told, Berry would get 178 yards that day. Our defensive back, Carl Karilivacz, tried to contain him, stopping just short of aggravated assault. But no matter what he did, or what adjustments Landry made, nothing worked. We had defensive "keys" that we thought would befuddle their offense. Unitas and Berry had devised their own counter keys. We were the ones being baffled. Before we knew it, their Colts were on our thirteen yard line and the clock was tick-tick-ticking toward the final gun.

SUDDEN DEATH

The Colts' kicker, Steve Myrha, hustled out on to the field for a twenty-yard field goal attempt. I was on the sideline, kneeling down behind him. He had a chip shot, but the fates intervened. He shanked it to the right. In that era, the uprights weren't nearly as high as they are now. You couldn't always tell if close kicks were really good or not. In addition, the officials did not stand under the goal post as they do now. The official standing behind me—about twenty-five yards away from the play—called it good. I disagreed, as if it mattered.

A small part of that ball may have gone over the upright, but not the majority of it. But that was a moot point. The game was tied 17–17 with seven seconds left. Back then, if a regular season game ended in a tie, it was counted as a tie. But we had to decide a championship here, and there had never been a sudden-death title game in NFL history. We were breaking new ground.

When the clock ran out, I was sitting next to Kyle Rote on the bench. "What's next?" I asked.

"I think we gotta play some more," he said.

TELEVISION DRUNK-OUT

The network broadcasting the game, NBC, had already pulled its wires and connections when regulation time ran out. When they realized the game was going into overtime, they unleashed the magic of television. They got one of their technicians to act like he was drunk and run out on the field to stall for time. Security guards were making a sport of chasing him around while NBC was frantically plugging things back in. It was a glorious moment in television sportscasting history.

Finally the network frivolity ended, and the officials told both benches we were going to toss another coin and start all over again. There were to be no timeouts, unlike in modern overtimes, which was bad news since we were feeling like we'd been dragged across ten miles of dirt road. But the game must go on.

We won the toss. They kicked off and the fun began. We were moving the ball well, but not as good as we thought. On third down with short yardage, Gifford appeared to make first down at midfield. But the officials took a measure and we came up inches short. To this day, Gifford claims it was a bad spot. It may have been. Once again, moot point. We had to punt, and Chandler put them inside their twenty yard line.

We never touched the ball again on offense. Unitas engineered an eighty-three yard drive, and Ameche plunged in from the one yard line. Eight minutes into the NFL's first overtime game, we were beaten 23–17. It was the league's longest game ever at the time, and some, including NFL Commissioner Bert Bell, would call it the "greatest game ever played."

I disagree. I think we were lucky to be in it. But in a sense, it was a watershed moment for the NFL. The game attracted a record number of television viewers, reaching more U.S. households than any previous sporting event. Professional football gained respect and millions of fans with that single game.

COACHING CHANGES

After the 1958 season ended, we lost our unmatched pair of coaching geniuses. Lombardi left for his first head-coaching job with the struggling Green Bay Packers. They'd earned a reputation as perpetual losers, but everyone knew Lombardi would change that.

Landry left, too. He joined Tex Schramm, who had given up a job as an assistant director of sports at CBS to become general manager of the upstart Dallas Cowboys franchise. Tex tapped Landry as his head coach. As usual, Tex knew what he was doing. Under Landry, the Cowboys would have twenty consecutive winning seasons—from 1966 to 1985—winning thirteen divisional titles, five conference championships, and two Super Bowls. Before Landry went off to become an NFL legend, he took time to call me from his apartment in our hotel.

"Summerall, I'd like to talk to you," he said.

You didn't turn down a call from Landry, even if he was no longer your coach. Though he was going to Dallas, Landry said there were a couple of kicking tips that he wanted to leave with me. It was a classy thing for him to do. He'd noticed a couple of tendencies in my kicking, and he suggested a few adjustments. He also told me that I should never practice without someone who understood kicking watching me. It was too easy to develop bad habits.

"You may beat me someday on account of this, but I still wanted you to know before I left," Landry told me.

It was great advice from a master coach. My kicking percentages improved over the rest of my career because I followed Landry's tips. I even used one of Landry's tips to kick a game-tying field goal against his Cowboys a few years later.

I didn't remind him. And he didn't ask.

DEER FISHING

When the football season ended, Kathy and I returned with our daughter, Susan, to Lake City. It was good to get lost in chores and a simpler life.

It wasn't all work. My cousin Mike and I had stayed close, and we entertained each other many nights, and even a few days. Our favorite hangout was a small fishing cabin near the mouth of the Suwannee River where it runs into the Gulf of Mexico. That cabin, which we still have today, offered a peaceful respite from the paramilitary world of professional football, and from the rigors of farming.

Of course, there were moments of high drama, too. We were on the river trying to scare up some redfish early one morning. Feeling a little hung over, we sipped brandy to get our body chemistries back into equilibrium. Our lazy morning was interrupted when we saw something flapping in the water. Through the double haze of the river's mist and brain fog, it looked like some huge waterfowl struggling to stay afloat. It could have been a great blue heron—or a whooping crane or a pterodactyl, for all we could tell.

We trolled over to see what it was, and we were surprised to discover that it was actually a male deer with a nice set of antlers swimming across the inlet, maybe in search of a friendly doe. The redfish weren't cooperating, so I suggested that venison might be an alternate menu choice. Mike was game, or so it seemed. He offered to pull the boat up close to the swimming deer so that his favorite cousin could leap out and somehow fish the deer out of the water. Maybe he was kidding, but for some reason—I wouldn't discount the brandy—it seemed like a perfectly sane idea to me.

I guess our game plan was then to knock the deer over the head with a paddle, toss it in the boat, kill it, and clean it. Looking back, the two of us were no match for Landry and Lombardi—or Abbott and Costello, for that matter. We eased up next to the wild-eyed deer, which was not pleased to have his morning swim interrupted. I had delusions of bull-dogging the buck like a rodeo cowboy. For reasons lost to the ages, I jumped out of the boat. I think it was somewhere in midair that it dawned on me: *this is no Bambi.* It had a very broad back, a thick neck, and, upon closer inspection, a formidable rack of antlers.

When I landed beside him in the waist-deep water, the deer responded to my bulldogging efforts by kicking me mercilessly with his powerful legs and sharp hooves. Forget all you've ever read about deer being shy woodland creatures. If they are, we'd paddled up on the world's only rogue killer buck. The only thing that saved me from having my heart hooved out of my chest was the pair of thick denim farmer coveralls I'd worn, which gave me extra protection. But even the thick jeans were being shredded. Even then, the deer didn't let up. He was set on slicing me to ribbons.

Somehow I came up with a professional underwater wrestling move and heaved the deer into the boat with my unprepared cousin. Apparently, Mike hadn't been taking notes because the deer kicked him silly and then began knocking our gear overboard. This was rapidly turning into "Titanic on the Suwannee."

Suddenly I lost all taste for venison and decided to end the deer slayer boat ride.

"Mike, let's get this son of a buck out of here." With that, we pushed Bucky overboard.

The deer wasn't even winded. He looked rather cocky, in fact. He swam for shore, antlers held high, to continue his love quest. Abbott and Costello sat in the boat, too exhausted and bloodied to move. Our clothes were slashed to shreds. Our tackle and other gear was floating down-stream. The only equipment that remained in our boat was the motor. We vowed to never again fish for deer.

TEAM LEADER

Kathy and I had a little more to pack when we returned to the Bronx for the 1959 season with the Giants. Our first son, Jay, joined little Susie in the backseat. It would be three years before we completed the family with Kyle, who was named after the Giants' team captain, Kyle Rote. I wasn't alone in my admiration. Eight Giants players named their sons after Kyle, and years later I learned that one player even had a grandson named after him—that was the sort of impression our team captain had made on us, and on our families.

The term *Renaissance man* barely does justice to this brilliant athlete, gentle soul, and big thinker. Michelangelo may have been the first true Renaissance man, but he was never a college All-American. Kyle mastered multitasking before the term was invented. When most of us were going out to drink beer or to socialize, Kyle stayed home and wrote his weekly broadcast report for WNEW radio in New York. He also served as the first elected president of the NFL Players Association—after founding it. Kyle was an accomplished pianist and songwriter who wrote the Giants' fight song. In his spare time, he published two volumes of poetry, wrote two football guides, and was such an accomplished oil painter that his works were shown in museums around the country. He had a mind that lacked an off-switch. One of his many inventions was a blanket with weighted corners that didn't blow away at picnics.

His athletic abilities were legendary even on a team that would go down in sports history for its depth of talent. If somebody brought a Ping-Pong table to training camp, Kyle would beat all comers, and he did it with a smile on his face. One year, for some reason a clown showed up at training camp with a unicycle. He challenged us to try and ride it. Nobody could—except Kyle, who started peddling it around like he'd been doing it for years.

Kyle's accomplishments on the field were equally impressive. In college he kicked a punt eighty-four yards during the 1949 Cotton Bowl. In a game against Notre Dame, he ran for 115 yards, threw for 146 more, and scored all three SMU touchdowns. He played varsity baseball, ran track, and hit .347 in twenty-three minor league games before reporting to the Giants training camp as the NFL's number-one draft choice.

Kyle started out as a running back for the Giants, and he probably would have run straight into the Pro Football Hall of Fame if as a rookie he hadn't stepped in a hole and torn up his knee. The injury was more severe than most people realized. It would have ended the careers of many players. But Kyle was better on one leg than most people with two. At Landry's advice, he switched to the wide receiver position, where he wouldn't take such a pounding. At first they tried taping up his leg like a mummy, but he couldn't stand playing like that. He wore no tape at all during his final two years in the league—and scored seventeen touchdowns in that stretch. In his final year, he had 805 yards as a receiver.

If Kyle had been able to play with two good knees, he probably would have been unstoppable. He was also the guy we went to for guidance on career and personal issues because of his principles and his common sense. Kyle served as our captain for eight years and was unquestionably the natural leader of a team that did not lack strong personalities. He wasn't perfect, of course, and that made him all the more admirable. At one point, he got involved in a bad business deal; as I recall, everyone bailed out on the debt—except Kyle. He scrimped and saved and sacrificed until he paid off everything that he owed. And then we all went out dancing. I can still see the joy in his eyes as he and his wife hit the dance floor to the Burt Bacharach tune "One Less Bell to Answer."

SEASON OF '59

Our team of great players added even more depth for the 1959 season. We had three strong quarterbacks in Charlie Conerly, Don Henrich, and

George Shaw; we picked up a fourth after the Steelers cut him. Jack Kemp was a strong-armed quarterback out of little Occidental College. He'd been drafted in the seventeenth round and struggled to find a place in the league. By the time he got to the Bronx to join the Giants, there were no rooms in the inn. So he and his wife and their baby had to live down the hall from us in a studio apartment at the Concourse Plaza Hotel. They had a hot plate and a minifridge.

Kathy and I got to be good friends with Jack and his wife, Joanne. They'd invite us over to their tiny room for dinner, and afterward the four of us would get down on our knees in the bathroom, hunch over the bathtub, and wash the dishes. Such was the glamorous life of a pro football player.

Jack didn't get much of a shot with the Giants, but after bouncing around a bit, he did all right for himself. He later became an All-Star for the San Diego Chargers and the Buffalo Bills before retiring to serve in Congress. He was Bob Dole's vice presidential running mate in 1996. He also served as secretary of Housing and Urban Development, where I'm sure he campaigned to put more dishwashers in studio apartments across the country.

In 1959, Frank Gifford led the team in both rushing and receiving as he'd done the previous three years. We beat the Browns two more times. I was thirty scores for thirty attempts in extra points, and twenty for twenty-nine in field goals. My career high that year—a total of ninety points on the season—was second only to Paul Hornung at Green Bay, who ran for seven touchdowns and kicked for Lombardi. We ended the 1959 season with four straight wins and a 10–2 record, capturing the NFL East by three games. The Baltimore Colts were still tough. They managed to fight off a good Bears team to capture the West Division by a single game, setting up a title game rematch.

This time we had to go to Baltimore and play them on their turf. The Colts opened the scoring again, with Unitas hitting Lenny Moore with a sixty-yard pass. I was in a groove, kicking three consecutive field goals of twenty-three, thirty-seven, and twenty-three yards—one in each of the first three quarters. The thirty-seven yarder, which I kicked just before halftime, was similar to the controversial one Steve Myrha booted in the playoff game against us the previous year. I pushed it a little, and it sailed over the upright, though not directly. I wasn't sure it was good, but I turned around to the official and thrust both my arms straight up in the air, like I had not a doubt in the world that it was as good as gold.

I should have taken up acting right then and there. The official looked at me and bought my act completely. He signaled "good." Players and coaches on the Colts' sidelines went berserk. I thought their big tackle, Gino Marchetti, was going to assassinate the entire officiating team. "That wasn't good!" he screamed. "That wasn't good!"

They didn't have instant replay or reviews back then. But there were enough second thoughts about it later that the following year they raised the goal posts higher.

After that drama, we managed to edge out to a slim 9–7 lead into the fourth period. Early in the final quarter, the Colts stopped Webster on fourth-down-and-inches, and their offense responded by engineering a touchdown drive, with Unitas sweeping around the right end for a touchdown like Quasimodo on a keeper. Then the Colts' defensive back, Johnny Sample, picked off a couple of Conerly passes, one for a touchdown, and the rout was on. Baltimore jumped out to a 31–9 lead, and we scored a meaningless last-second touchdown to lose 31–16. The Giants brass had expected a championship and didn't get one. It was a disappointment, but this team was so solid we immediately began looking forward to taking another shot at the championship in the 1960 NFL season.

Even before we returned to training camp, we lost Jack Kemp to the new American Football League draft. It turned out to be a good move for Jack, who was elected captain of the new San Diego Chargers, which I'm sure qualified him for a place fully stocked with modern appliances. He didn't miss much upon leaving the Giants. We disappointed ourselves and everyone else in town by going 6-4-2 in the 1960 regular season and missing the postseason altogether. It was even more demoralizing because we finished just a half game ahead of my old team, the Cardinals, who had moved their team to St. Louis after the 1959 season and found new life in the Budweiser fold. The 1960 championship trophy went to the Philadelphia Eagles, who beat Lombardi's Green Bay Packer team renovation in progress by four points. It was the Eagles first NFL title since 1949.

FINAL FLING

My career was winding down, and the seasons seemed to come right on top of each other. Before I knew it we were back for the 1961 season, the first featuring the NFL's expanded fourteen-game schedule.

Allie Sherman came in as our new rookie head coach. We also picked up veteran quarterback Y. A. Tittle, which relegated my old roomie Conerly—the oldest player in the league at age forty (he claimed)—to a backup role. That caused a little resentment and added to the uncharacteristic dissension in our ranks. Maybe we were all just getting old and cranky. Tittle was as accurate as Layne—perhaps more so. He threw seventeen touchdown passes for us that year. I chipped in some points, too, making forty-six straight extra-point attempts. We may have been old and cranky, but we were still able to generate some offense. We ran neck-and-neck with the Eagles all year. Then we finished the season by beating them and tying Cleveland to win the division by a half game. Our record was a very respectable 10-3-1.

The only thing between the championship and us was a pack of cheeseheads led by one of the greatest coaches of all time. The Packers were back with a vengeance. They rolled up almost four hundred points during the season, and then won their division with time to spare. They dominated that season, racking up more rushing yards, more first downs, and more touchdowns than any other NFL team. Green Bay had beaten us by three points in Milwaukee earlier in the season, so we had that to think about as we prepared to face them in the NFL title game. It didn't help that the game was New Year's Eve day in Green Bay, which was somewhere north of the North Pole, judging from the climate we encountered.

Remember, this was before sideline heaters and global warming. I think it was before thermal underwear, too. Parts of me are still thawing out forty-five years later. That game was supposed to pit two high-powered offenses against one another, but only one showed up. And it wasn't us.

Both teams went scoreless in the first quarter, but Green Bay answered the bell and we didn't. Bart Starr, a man whose last name said it all, threw touchdown passes to Boyd Dowler, Paul Hornung, and Ron Kramer, putting the Pack on top 24–0 at halftime. We never warmed up. In the second half, Kyle Rote dropped a sure touchdown pass. Green Bay intercepted our master quarterback, Y. A. Tittle, four times, beating him up unmercifully. The Giants went down in a big ugly pile, 37–0. Lombardi had led Green Bay to their first title, and the Packers kept the Giants from hiring him away by signing him to a five-year contract. It was a good move on their part. Under Lombardi, the Packers dominated pro football in the 1960s, winning six division titles, five NFL Championships, and the first two Super Bowls; they posted a record of 98–30.

I didn't stick around to watch. I was a veteran past my prime, and my aching knees and back reminded me of that fact every morning and night. I had a wife and two children, and professional football wasn't offering me much of a future—at least, not on the playing field.

CHAPTER FIVE

THE GIFT OF GAB

I GOT A GLIMPSE OF MY FUTURE BEFORE THE 1960 SEASON, AND IT wasn't in football or farming. I was hanging around a Manhattan hotel room on an off day when I intercepted a phone call for my former roommate Charlie Conerly. It was someone from WCBS-880 Radio in New York. I offered to take a message. "Remind him that he's supposed to come over to CBS this afternoon to read an audition script for a five-minute radio program," the caller said.

"I'll be glad to tell him," I said.

I was preparing to hang up the phone when I thought I heard the caller say something else. I put the phone back to my ear, and he asked me a question: "What are you doing this afternoon?"

That seemed strange, but I played along.

"I'm just going to hang out with the guys, maybe go to a movie or drink a few beers somewhere."

"Well, why don't you come along with Charlie, and give it a shot, too?"

I felt like the starlet discovered by a Hollywood producer at the soda fountain. So I tagged along with Charlie. As it turned out, there were four of us from the Giants called to audition for a five-minute weekly sports-broadcast job. The fantastic foursome consisted of Alex Webster, Kyle

Rote, Charlie, and me. Our golden boy teammate, Frank Gifford, had been doing the weekly broadcast, which was an insider report on Giants football similar to what Phil Rizzuto of the Yankees did during baseball season. But Gifford had signed a promotional deal with Lucky Strike cigarettes, and the radio show had picked up competitor Camel as its sponsor. So CBS needed someone to replace Gifford or face a flameout from the sponsor. Kyle was already doing a radio show on an independent station, but he wanted the network job. At first it seemed like I'd wandered into a beauty contest uninvited, but my competitive juices got to churning. Whether it was playing football or talking about it, I wanted to win.

I was surprisingly at home behind the microphone. My grandmother read to me all the time when I was a boy, and reading aloud in a radio sound booth came naturally to me. It was as if her voice had trained mine. The folks at CBS apparently saw that I had a knack for it, because the walk-on got the position. After getting beat up on the football field and working in the watermelon patch, it was an appealing line of work. The radio pros told me that I had a naturally rich voice that carried well over the airwaves. Later it sunk in that, for all of my athletic gifts, it was my gift of gab that proved to be my greatest asset.

SPORTSCASTING CALL

I did the CBS spots during the 1960 and 1961 football seasons; I thought I'd died and gone to heaven. Getting paid to talk about sports seemed too much fun to be legal. Then, just as I was seriously contemplating hanging up my spikes to pursue a broadcasting career, Kyle Rote called me in Florida with a tip that led to one of my life's greatest opportunities. It seemed that former Chicago Bears quarterback Johnny Lujack was being forced to quit his postfootball career as the CBS television analyst for New York Giant broadcasts. Ford Motor Company had signed on to sponsor the Giants' games for the 1962 season. That posed a problem for Lujack, because he had married into the family that owned one of the most prominent Chevrolet dealerships in the country. Ford bumped the Chevy man from the program.

Kyle Rote once again proved himself to be a first-class guy and a great friend by calling me as soon as he heard the news. "I think it would be a good idea for you to talk to CBS about that opening," Kyle said.

FORTUNE SMILES

At that point in my life, I tended to take wonderful moments like that in stride, as if they were simply meant to be. I never stopped to wonder why my life had been blessed with so many great opportunities. I thanked Kyle, of course, but my gratitude didn't extend much further up the ladder. Mostly, I was just so eager to get on with my life—and so busy trying to make things happen—that I didn't pause to marvel at the amazing grace with which I was moving from one career to the next. Of course, at that point, nobody knew if it was going to work out. More than a few people didn't think it would.

I followed Kyle's advice and made a call to CBS in New York to set up a meeting. Then I headed for Manhattan on the first plane I could catch. My initial appointment was with Bill MacPhail, head of the CBS sports department. He let me know there was an obstacle that had to be cleared before our discussions could go beyond the preliminary stages if I wanted the sportscasting job.

"We can't even talk to you until you retire from the NFL," he said, citing agreements made with the league about active players becoming broadcasters.

No problem. I grabbed a cab and headed across town to find Giants owner Wellington Mara so I could end my playing career.

Mr. Mara had his own thoughts. "I don't want you to retire," he said. "And I don't think you can make this broadcasting business pay. But if that's what you want to do, I won't stand in your way. You won't have to retire first. Just tell them you're retired and see what they say. Then get back to me."

Back I went to CBS as he instructed.

MacPhail took the bait. "Okay, we're interested," he said. Then he went looking for his boss to get approval to hire me.

His boss gave the thumbs up. Before I knew it, I was sitting with one of their head bean counters negotiating a salary. Well, negotiating might be the wrong term.

"Our best offer is going to be $325 a game for fourteen games a year," he said. "But we'll pay for your expenses to commute from Florida to wherever the Giants are playing."

"Well, that's a start," I said. I figured I could still teach and farm during the week back in Lake City if that didn't cover the bills. So I retired after ten NFL seasons, 563 points, and three championship bids—all failed. I'd had a good career as a professional athlete. I'd certainly had my share of fun. I'd met some terrific people and many lifelong friends. But I'd reached the point on the field where my mind was sending me to places where my body could not go. My knees were screaming "retirement," and I needed to find a job that didn't involve collisions with stampeding herds of three-hundred-pound men, or toting watermelons until my hands were raw.

TELEVISION TIME

My luck was incredible, my timing impeccable. Television was just coming into its own, and sports-broadcasting was its driving force. The United States was entering into a period of unprecedented prosperity and growth. That meant more leisure time, more spending money, and a television sports audience that couldn't seem to get enough.

Football was the biggest draw for television audiences. It was a sport made for this medium. The field was divided into easy-to-see segments, and the play-by-play flow of the game allowed plenty of time for commercials and tidbits from the announcers.

The creation of the American Football League in 1960 had upped the ante. CBS had dominated NFL coverage up to that point. The new league signed a five-year contract with NBC. It was the first television deal for a league in which the profits were divided equally among member teams. NBC introduced innovations like on-field cameras and putting microphones on players during games. Within a couple of years, CBS signed a similar deal with the NFL. Over the next few years, the annual fee for broadcasting games skyrocketed from less than $5 million to $36 million by 1965. I had definitely walked into a growth industry at just the right time.

I began working the Giants games as an on-air analyst with play-by-play man Chris Schenkel, who'd been one of the early voices of NFL network broadcasts and was rolling along on top of the industry. He had been broadcasting Giants football since 1952. Chris called every one of the NFL Championship games I played in, including that now-legendary "Greatest Game Ever Played." He had also been the first to do the Masters Tournament on network television. Chris was a dapper dresser, always in a coat and tie, perfectly turned out from his shoelaces to the little stickpin on his collar. His attention to detail included doing his homework before every game. And he was where he was supposed to be, when he was supposed to be there.

His first bit of advice to me: "If you're going to have to fill ten minutes on the air, prepare for a half-hour. If you're going to have a half-hour, prepare for four hours." He also stressed that television was a visual medium and that I didn't need to tell people what they could already see. It was basic but useful advice that I applied throughout my broadcasting career.

Chris also had a great feel for the game and for the entire wide world of sports. We'd rendezvous for the weekend wherever the Giants were playing, and then spend hours preparing for the broadcasts. We'd go over the rosters, bone up on each team's injuries, their offensive and defensive tendencies, their position in the standings, the personalities of the players and the coaches—everything we could think of that might be of interest to the fans. We did not have what I later learned were the customary production meetings with the producer and director. Chris was such a pro that he handled those jobs, too. He was a great teacher and role model for me, a proud graduate of the Schenkel School of Broadcasting.

Chris was also no slouch in the social aspects of the broadcast game. He plugged me into his sports and broadcast network of contacts, made sure I got to meet the major players in all departments, and provided me with personal tours of their watering holes and hangouts. Chris was a charming guy with a smooth, deep voice and a great sense of style. The knot in his tie was always tight, but he was warm and engaging to everyone who approached him. His work ethic was matched by a fondness for playing late into the night. His was a very civilized, very social, and very seductive lifestyle.

I was definitely the junior partner in our collaboration, but Chris never made me feel like the trainee. He was positive about everything and everyone, and he gracefully carried the broadcast while I got invaluable on-the-job training. I missed out on some basic things—for example, he knew so much that he didn't have to track down coaches and players prior to the game to get their insights. Most of them couldn't tell him anything he didn't know. CBS banked on his broad knowledge, and since I had game bruises that were still healing, I contributed some fresh insights.

I was a rookie in the broadcasting leagues, so I didn't give up my weekday job. I was still teaching back in Lake City during the week and working with Chris on weekends. Still, I was even called upon to do some broadcast work in my teaching job. On Friday, November 22, 1963, Principal P. A. Browning summoned me to his office and asked me to make an announcement over the school's public address system. President John F. Kennedy had been shot in Dallas.

Like everyone else, I was so stunned that for me the moment was frozen in time. The days that followed were also unforgettable. Chris and I were scheduled to do a Giants-Cardinals game in New York that weekend. There was a lot of discussion in the NFL headquarters over whether the game would even be played, given the national tragedy, but the bosses told us to come to New York just in case. We spent Saturday going through the motions of preparing because there had still been no decision made. The entire city of New York, and much of the world around it, was still in shock.

Everywhere you went there was this funereal hush. Everyone was mesmerized by the events unfolding on television; talk of anything else— including a football game—seemed frivolous and disrespectful. On Saturday, the NFL announced it would allow the game to be played, but early Sunday morning CBS decided not to broadcast it. Chris and I went to Yankee Stadium, mostly because we didn't know what else to do. We were sitting in the office of a Giants executive, watching as Kennedy's assassin, Lee Harvey Oswald, was being brought into the Dallas Police Department. Suddenly, this guy in a dark hat and suit appeared out of nowhere and shot him.

It was the most stunning thing I had ever seen. We couldn't speak or think for several minutes as we watched the police take away the fatally wounded Oswald and his attacker, whom we later learned was a nightclub owner, Jack Ruby. Later, we went into the broadcast booth and watched the game, but our hearts and our minds were focused on other things, wondering where our country was headed. John F. Kennedy had been such a dynamic and dashing president. The future had seemed so bright and promising. Now, it seemed so uncertain.

TOAST OF THE TOWN

Shortly after that, my own career took a turn, but it proved to be a good one. As we were preparing for a Giants broadcast, Chris Schenkel tipped me off to a sports director's job opening in New York. They'd offered it to Chris, but he preferred to stay on the road. He told me to call a sales guy at WCBS radio in Manhattan, who invited me to audition by writing a brief sports show and then performing it on the air.

I'd been working toward this sort of job for four years, but I was a wreck going into it. The adrenalin was flowing, and I had a bad case of motor mouth, speaking so fast that I wrapped up the entire show two minutes early. Fortunately, I had a pro, a staff announcer named Hal Simms, working with me. He quickly plugged in a couple of public-service announcements to fill the time, saving my way-ahead behind.

Despite the rough ending, WCBS, the flagship station of the radio network, offered me the job. This time I was prepared to do some hardnosed negotiating.

"How much is this gonna pay? Because I'm pretty happy with what's going on in my life now," I said, playing it cool.

"We think you can move up pretty quickly, but the starting salary is $75,000."

"How soon do I start?"

HOG HEAVEN

Seventy-five grand was major money for that time, even in New York. There was even more gold to be mined if my radio segments attracted big-time national sponsors.

I used some of my new earnings to invest in a bunch of pigs with a high-school buddy back in Lake City who'd always wanted to be a hog farmer. Now I could afford to be an absentee owner, which was a very good thing; if Kathy got one whiff of that business, she'd make me throw the clothes away.

After the Giants game that weekend, I flew back to Florida and told Kathy about the offer. I was expected to start as sports director of WCBS on January fourth, at the end of the season.

I could hear her brain working over the logistics. "Does that mean we've got to move to New York?" she asked.

She was not thrilled. Lake City was her home. Her family was there. She'd hoped that once I retired, we could move there permanently and settle down to a more normal family life. Instead, I was moving her back to the big city, away from family and friends, with three young children to look after.

I had not saved enough for a house in the New York market, but I had the next best thing—a friend whose father was a Connecticut banker. He helped me to get a loan so we could get a house in Stamford, which was about an hour by train to the radio station in Manhattan. When in the winter of 1964 we headed north from Lake City, the chill in the air wasn't entirely due to the climate.

AIR SUMMERALL

No longer was I under the wing of Chris Schenkel. I was flying solo in this new job. I did it all, with some assistance from a researcher. Even though I was working for the primary radio satellite of the CBS broadcast mothership, my job wasn't much different from that of the radio sports guy working high-school games in Dubuque. I took my little tape recorder to team practices, interviewed the stars and coaches, brought the tapes back, edited them, wrote the shows, and engineered each day's broadcast. I'd received training in the high end from Schenkel; now I was learning the nitty-gritty stuff on the ground level.

Still, it beat lugging melons to market.

Since I was doing all sports, all the time, I found myself knocking on the Yankees' door as baseball season was warming up. I was a rookie in radio, but the connections I made as an athlete paid big dividends. I only knew one Yankee. But what a Yankee—Mickey Mantle! I tagged my old Yankee Stadium locker-mate for my first baseball interview.

He didn't like doing this sort of thing, but Mickey was too good a guy to turn me down. He knew I was nervous, so he gave me one of the warmest, most gracious interviews he'd ever done. He made me look good.

Once I had him on tape, the other Yankees made themselves available. It took me a few tries, but I even got to the notoriously shy Roger Maris, who'd grown even more averse to doing media interviews since hitting his record-breaking sixty-first home run in 1961. Some had turned on him because he'd broken Babe Ruth's hallowed homerun record and upstaged Mickey, who was most fans' favorite Yankee.

Of course, Maris didn't help himself by lashing out at the fans and his critics and blaming the media. When I asked him about his goals for the year, he was curt: "I have some goals, but I'm not gonna tell you what they are."

I tried to protect him by asking if he was sure he wanted me to use those quotes, but Maris wasn't one to put up a false front. He had a chip on his shoulder, and he didn't mind wearing it in public. "No, that's the way I feel. Play it."

Had I been a veteran broadcaster, I might have been able to convince him to do a more upbeat interview. But I didn't want to cross him, so I put those comments on the air. It caused a minor media stir, riling the fans and reinforcing what many now feel was an unfair portrayal of Maris as a villain. He felt he was misunderstood, and maybe he was. But he didn't help his own case.

TALKER IN TRAINING

Thanks to my earlier training and my personal connections to many of the athletes and coaches, I quickly came to feel at home in the new job. Like most athletes, I had to work at being a better listener so that my interviews flowed. My tutor in that department was an all-ears all-star, the legendary Art Linkletter, who was then hosting *House Party*, which CBS ran for twenty-five years on both television and radio.

The most popular feature of his show was the segment in which he interviewed a group of kids. It became his "Kids Say the Darndest Things" franchise. Athletes were hard enough to interview, and kids could be impossible—but Linkletter was a master. I marveled at how he drew them out. He told me that the key wasn't what you said, it was how well you listened. "It doesn't have anything to do with what you're thinking, you have to listen to them to understand what they have going in their minds. If you don't listen closely, you'll be in trouble."

The other new aspect of my job, writing the shows, was less of a challenge because I'd always been a big reader of the sports pages and books—and I'd spent many hours listening to the radio with my grandmother. So writing and reporting for broadcasts came naturally to me. The top news anchors at WCBS, Lou Adler and Ken Banghart, were generous with their guidance, and that helped as well.

The advertisers must have liked what I was doing. My four-minute sports segment was broadcast every hour during the afternoon, and it was packed with commercials for national brands. The advertiser support bumped my salary to $125,000 a year, which definitely helped pay the mortgage and my train fare.

My network bosses included two legendary top dogs, chairman William Paley and president Frank Stanton. These brilliant men had their eccentricities, especially Stanton, a man of many different shades—all of them brown. He had a brown limousine, brown suits, brown ties, and brown shoes. When he sent me comments on my shows, they always arrived on little brown-tinted notepaper. He wasn't much for wordy dissections. If he liked a show, his brown note featured a hand-drawn smiling face. If he thought I stunk it up, I got a brown frown face. Most of the time, I got the smiley faces; the "brown buzz" was that the big bosses thought I had a bright future in broadcasting.

When another broadcast Hall of Famer, Arthur Godfrey, left his WCBS early morning variety show to do television, the top brass teamed me up with his replacement, Jack Sterling, who had been the "ringmaster" of the top Saturday morning cartoon show *The Big Top*. I joined his show to do sports during the premium morning-drive time slot. He also had traffic and weather reports, recorded music, and even live bands. My sports segments increased from four minutes each hour to three minutes every half hour. They also tapped me to do sports segments for CBS television, so I was juggling a lot but loving it.

A WINK AND A NOD

After just a few months as the sportscaster on the morning show, I got an unexpected bump up the ladder. The station manager, Tom Swofford, called me into his office, shut the door, closed the blinds, and announced that I was part of a secret plan. "Pat, the more I listen to the morning show, it's apparent that this is becoming 'The Pat Summerall Show' instead of 'The Jack Sterling Show.' I want you to take it over fulltime."

I was shocked.

"You gotta be kidding! I don't know anything about New York traffic. I don't know anything about the weather. I don't know anything about music. I know sports—but that's all I know."

"We'll teach you," he said. "I want you to take the whole four-and-a-half hour morning show, beginning at 5:30."

Before I could protest any further, he said the magic words.

"We're gonna make you a rich man, Pat."

Although Sterling may have suspected something was brewing, he knew nothing about the plan to replace him. Swofford wanted to keep it that way. So, to prepare me for the job, WCBS sent me to Los Angeles for two weeks of training under Wink Martindale, the former rock and roll radio deejay who had been the morning man at CBS affiliate KFWB before becoming a game show host extraordinaire.

"You can't tell anybody where you're going or what you're doing," Swofford told me.

"Well, I have to tell my wife," I said.

"Okay, tell your wife, but nobody else."

So off I flew to L.A. on my secret mission to work with Wink. He showed me the ropes for hosting a morning show, down to the best form for pointing at the weather map. It was a good introduction, but I really wasn't ready for prime time even after I returned. I told my station manager that I had some concerns about taking on such an enormous responsibility during such a crucial time slot.

"Don't worry, Pat, we'll surround you with staff. We'll have somebody pick the music for you. The only thing you have to concern yourself with is the weather and the traffic."

The traffic thing really had me worried. The only knowledge I had of New York traffic came from watching it from the window of my commuter train. The station manager told me I'd pick it up as I went.

"We want you to start in two weeks," he said. "But don't tell anybody."

Before I could protest any further, he ran the numbers by me. My base salary was just the beginning. I was going to earn a cut from every commercial that aired during the show—and the advertising revenues for prime drive time were lucrative. The earning potential was in excess of $500,000 a year. For that kind of money I could learn to say, "Traffic is screwed up, so leave early or stay home" in six different languages.

SUPERMAN FLIES AMOK

Doing traffic wasn't as tough as I thought it would be. Our two helicopter pilots did most of the work. They fed me the bad news, and I passed it on and got all the credit. WCBS even wrapped a creative marketing campaign around my traffic coverage. The station had me pose in a Superman suit for a life-size poster, calling me "Super Summerall." They plastered the posters all over Manhattan—it got to be a little embarrassing. The station distributed even more of the posters to commuters, who would then put them on top of their cars if they broke down, signaling a need for help. Our chopper pilots would then spot the Super Summeralls and call for assistance to help the stranded motorists. The pilots took to calling their choppers the "Help-i-copters."

I could have used some real clones, given my ever-increasing workload. I was doing football games on the weekends, my morning show, and regular assignments for WCBS-TV and the television network. I was holding down three jobs. It was fun and exciting and even glamorous a lot of the time. Suddenly I was thrown into the arena with every celebrity passing through the city; actors, singers, comedians—they all ended up on my show. I spent an hour every morning with guests in the studio, including the memorable fan dancer Sally Rand, who was then a little past her prime but still very game.

"Sally, I'm sorry we got you up so early. I know this is not on your regular schedule," I said on the air.

"Sweetheart, don't apologize," she responded. "A few years ago, you could have just rolled over and nudged me."

In my weekend television work, what went on off-camera was sometimes a lot wilder than what happened in the game. I was doing a postgame interview with quarterback Sonny Jurgensen shortly after he was traded from the Eagles to the Redskins in a controversial deal. Sonny had just blistered his old team's defense for thirty-five points. We were on a set near the field for the postgame show with Sonny. We were waiting for the cameras to roll when Sonny's old Eagles' receiver, split-end Tommy McDonald, walked onto the set in uniform. Just as the only camera on the set began to roll for the live interview, McDonald squatted down behind it, pulled down his pants, and mooned us. He held that full moon position through the whole interview. Sonny and I tried to keep straight faces. We didn't do very well.

I was finding my new job fascinating and incredibly demanding. The social aspects were every bit as alluring, but something had to give. I was running at full speed, day and night. Sadly, Kathy and our kids got the worst of the deal. While I was gallivanting with celebrities and entertaining the masses, Kathy was running the show at home without much support from her celebrity husband. I slept in two different shifts.

During the week I got up at 3:30 a.m. and was done with my radio gig at 10:00 a.m. About the time everyone else was just settling into work, I was ready to play. So I'd go out to lunch, which generally included a couple cocktails to take the edge off. Then I'd go home and sleep off the cocktails, get up, have dinner, and do some more work. I hardly saw Kathy and the kids because I was working, traveling, partying, and sleeping such odd hours. My weekends were usually loaded with game assignments or reporting gigs.

The money was flowing in, but financial concerns were replaced by a bankrupt relationship. I stayed on this calamity course for a year and a half before WCBS decided to retool and go to an all-news format, which relieved me of the morning show duty. I gladly returned to covering sports, this time for television. My old teammate Frank Gifford, who had retired after the 1964 season, was handling the Giants game analysis with Jack Whitaker, so the network assigned me to be analyst for Washington Redskins games, pairing me with Jim Gibbons.

Gibbons didn't know much about football at the time, but like Schenkel he was as smooth as silk and a master schmoozer and charmer.

He was very popular in Washington, and he showed me around town. I had developed a stronger work ethic during my morning-man stint, and I threw that energy into becoming more comfortable in front of the camera. I also got more serious about my analysis of game strategies. My competitive instincts drove me to be the best, so I worked hard at it. My partner and I hit the road every week, calling the Redskins' games for two years.

The new job allowed me to see my old friend Kyle Rote from time to time. Kyle had been the Giants backfield coach for two years after retiring from the game. He became the lead sports broadcaster with WNEW, a major independent radio station in New York. One day he confided that he had divorced his wife. I'd noticed that Kyle was drinking more and figured it was how he coped with the loss. He may have noticed the same about me.

THE WAY IT WAS

Social drinking was a big part of our schedule. There were a lot of hard-core drinkers in broadcasting, and near the head of the class was a flamboyant lawyer-turned-sportscaster named Howard Cosell. I'd met Howard in my playing days when he was starting out at ABC radio. He'd come into the locker room looking for human-interest stories or inside information on the teams. I was always polite with him, and we struck up a cordial relationship. It sounds silly, but I loved Howard for his mind. He radiated intelligence.

He also took himself and his job very seriously, and he didn't try to mask his resentment of ex-jocks in the broadcast booth. I didn't get his point. It seems to make more sense for an athlete to talk about sports than for a lawyer to talk about them. But I never argued the point with Howard, since he didn't seem to lump me in with the other ex-jocks. He was known for being abrasive and critical, but he never said an unkind thing to me.

We spent a lot of time together. Howard lived in Pound Ridge, New York, just up the hill from our place in Connecticut. We often rode the train home together, and we socialized with our wives together. Howard and I had a lot of heart-to-heart talks. He was a good listener and was truly concerned about the things going on in my life. He was, in short, a good and caring friend.

Howard was a world-class martini drinker. He could sit for hours with his tie knotted tightly, pounding down one martini after another, still looking very dignified. One night when he and his wife, Emmy, were over for dinner, I made him fourteen stiff martinis. Then he got up and made himself a couple more. I don't know how he was able to speak, much less stand. He must have had the constitution of an ox.

Even when drinking that hard, Howard stayed on good behavior as long as it was just him and a close friend or two. He sometimes got argumentative—like a trial lawyer—when the conversation turned to social concerns. He particularly hated racism and discrimination. His defense of Muhammad Ali brought him all kinds of hate mail and death threats. But he stood by Ali even when the New York State Boxing Commission stripped the champion of his title because Ali had claimed conscientious-objector status in the draft.

When there was a crowd, Howard liked to say things that stimulated the conversation, even if it meant purposely pushing someone's buttons. I heard him make the sort of racist comments that he hated just to get a conversation going. If someone dared to engage him verbally, Howard loved to wade in. He also didn't back down from physical confrontations, either.

When Howard drank in public, however, this complex man underwent a personality change that could be dramatic and sometimes scary. After working an Ernie Terrell fight in Houston, he and I were heading home on the same train, playing liar's poker in the bar car. Suddenly, the train lurched to a halt somewhere in the middle of the Bronx. We sat awhile without budging, and Howard lost what little patience he had.

"Let's get off this train, Pat," Howard said to me. "There's no telling how long we're going to be broken down. We'll find a cab and get somebody else to split the fare with us."

I doubted that the Bronx was teeming with cabs so late at night, but Howard's mind was made up. "I'll get a cab, you just find another rider to go with us," he said. With that, Howard walked off into the night.

A half hour later, he returned in the back of a taxi. I'd rustled up an advertising man who lived near us so we all piled in, leaving the train dead in its tracks. This was years before Howard became a controversial and nationally known sportscaster, but both the cab driver and our fellow passenger recognized Howard and me.

The advertising guy, who was in the backseat with Howard, made it clear that he was not a fan. He'd listened to Howard's broadcast of the fight that night, and he made some negative comments about it. Howard did not take kindly to being criticized in his own cab. The next thing I knew, they were swinging away, knocking the crap out of each other. Howard was all cut up, and blood was everywhere.

I ordered the driver to stop the cab before they killed each other.

Howard and his backseat critic were still shoving each other as we piled out of the car. The poor cab driver must have wondered what sort of maniacs he'd picked up in the Bronx. It wasn't often that I got to play the level-headed adult, but I separated the two brawlers and made Howard get in the front seat while I joined the ad guy in the back.

Howard got in without protest, then slumped over in the seat. His toupee fell off, and I could see a gash in his head. After we were rolling, he and his opponent calmed down and apologized to each other and to our driver.

"I overreacted and I shouldn't have. Whiskey was involved," the ad man said.

Howard also expressed his contrition.

Peace returned to the taxi. Finally, we reached our neighborhoods. The ad guy told the driver to stop and let him out so he could walk a block to his house. As he started to get out, the ad man turned and sucker-punched Howard in the back of the head! He hit Cosell so hard that Howard's head snapped forward and broke the cab's windshield, knocking him out cold. The ad guy then took off into the night. To this day, I don't know who he was.

Stunned, I asked the cab driver to take us to Howard's house. He was just regaining consciousness when we got there. His head was bleeding like crazy, and he had a scary lump on his forehead. I had to pull him out of the taxi and walk him to the front door. He was hugging my shoulder all the way. I rang the doorbell and his wife, Emmy, appeared.

"What in God's name happened?" she asked upon seeing her battered husband.

"Oh, nothing, just the usual trip home," I muttered.

I wound up feeling sucker punched, too. I got stuck with the whole cab fare, and the tip!

CHAPTER SIX

ADVENTURES ON THE AIR

THE FIRST SUPER BOWL, HELD ON JANUARY 15, 1967, WAS ORIGINALLY billed as the first AFL-NFL World Championship. The postseason game was created more or less as an experiment following the 1966 merger of the American and the National football leagues. The NFL teams, which considered themselves far superior to the AFL teams, were not much interested in participating. They thought whoever won the NFL title was the world champion. But the former AFL teams saw it as a chance to prove that they were as good as the more established league.

While the rival leagues struck a truce, NBC, which had broadcast the upstart AFL Championship in previous years, and CBS, which had broadcast the NFL Championship game, duked it out over this new championship game. They both wanted it, so they both did it. I was tapped to work it for CBS as an analyst before and after the game. But like almost everybody else, I had no idea that this game would serve as the beginning of a legendary series that would become a global event.

The sort of excitement you feel now was missing then; most people thought the AFC champs, the Kansas City Chiefs, were no match for Lombardi's Packers. The fans were staying away in droves. There were protests about the high price of the $12 tickets. Sponsors were not lining up to pay millions for commercial time. There weren't any huge corporate parties. They held it in Los Angeles, and we treated it like any game. We flipped a coin to see which network produced it. NBC won the flip, so Chet Simmons produced the game. Ray Scott and Jack Whitaker got the call to broadcast the game for CBS while Frank Gifford and I did the pre- and postgame analysis. The day and the event were full of surprises—especially for those of us who thought we knew everything.

In truth, I had some trepidation about working this "super" game, mostly because my old coach, Lombardi, and I already had clashed during the NFL Championship game. My CBS director had asked me to approach the Packers coach about interviewing some of his players during pregame warm-ups for the playoff game between Green Bay and the Rams. I knew that he asked me because everyone else was terrified of Lombardi. He had developed an intense distrust for the sports media. But like a good soldier, I went to him and made the request a week before the game.

He gave me a "no" and a "hell, no."

"You're not taking my players out of warm-ups," he said.

I knew that Lombardi appreciated tenacity, so I didn't give up. I kept asking him, reminding him of every good kick and decent tackle I'd ever made on his behalf as a player. Finally, I wore him down.

"Okay, okay. I don't really want to do it—it's just another foot in the door for you people. But just remember, I'm not a friend with you guys. We will do it, but only one player at a time, and for no more than five minutes," he said.

I took that as a yes.

Lombardi and I agreed that I could talk with Jerry Kramer, Boyd Dowler, and a couple of others for the warm-up interviews. I thanked him profusely. I may have genuflected and kissed his feet, I was that grateful.

On the day of the playoff game in arctic Green Bay, I walked out on the icy field and tapped Kramer on the shoulder as he was warming up.

I told him we had two minutes before the interview. Kramer nodded, but I saw him look nervously over my shoulder.

That was not a good sign.

I turned around, and there was Lombardi staring daggers at me. He marched over like General Patton preparing to do a slap down on a sloppy private. "What the hell are you doing here?" he demanded.

"Coach, we talked about this. You know, about interviewing the players."

If Lombardi remembered our earlier conversation, he was not letting on. "You are not doing anything like that! Get out of here—and get that camera out of here, too."

I hightailed it to the sidelines where I had to face yet another irate authority figure.

"What the hell happened?" my director said.

"We'd agreed to the interviews, but now he's telling me to get away from his players," I replied.

The director put his hands on his head in the international gesture for a brain about to explode in panic. "Patrick, think of everything you know about football and start saying it, because we've got eighteen minutes to fill!"

Remember, if I was known for anything as a broadcaster, it was brevity. So that may well have been the longest uninterrupted sideline soliloquy of my entire television career. Even I didn't know that I knew so much about the history of football. But as Michael Jordan would say years later: "Sometimes I amaze myself!"

When it came time for the first Super Bowl, I had to deal with Lombardi once again. His team won the NFL Division Championship; as far as the Packers were concerned, this Super Bowl thing was just a sideshow, an afterthought, and a waste of what should have been their off-season. In other words, they wanted nothing to do with more media interviews. Lombardi, who had always considered the media to be a fly in his soup, was even less enthused about doing interviews for this game.

Their Super Bowl opponent, on the other hand, was eager to do anything we asked. The former American Football League's Kansas City Chiefs were eager to prove that they could take on the NFL's top team. Most of us thought they didn't have a chance. But we played along with the Super Bowl idea because it meant more revenues for our networks.

It was an honor to be chosen to do the game, even if I was the sideline guy and not one of the broadcasters in the booth. And the first half of the game was exciting. Kansas City, led by former NFL reserve quarterback Len Dawson, proved to be much better than anyone had thought they would be against the Packers. Lombardi's Green Bay had a dynasty going with NFL Championships in 1961, 1962, 1965, and 1966, and they had a tremendous quarterback, Bart Starr.

Kansas City made two impressive drives early in the game, scoring a touchdown on the second one. Green Bay scrambled back and tied them, but just before half Kansas City got a field goal. The fact that Green Bay wasn't mopping up on Kansas City had everyone a little loopy at half time. That's the only explanation I can think of for what happened next.

When the second half started, our CBS team was ready to roll, so we did. But NBC missed the second half kickoff entirely because one of their broadcasters, Charlie Jones, was doing an interview with Bob Hope when it happened. When the referees learned that NBC had missed the kickoff, to the amazement of all they decided there would have to be a "rekick."

Incredibly, my director's voice came over my headset as I stood on Green Bay's sidelines, requesting that I ask Coach Lombardi if they would mind kicking off again.

My answer was absolutely not. There was no way I was going to get chewed out by Coach Lombardi on national television. "You'll have to find somebody else to tell him," I told my director.

They did, and the Packers went on to win what became known as the first Super Bowl. For me, it was the first of sixteen Super Bowl television broadcasts, and the only one in which I worked the sidelines instead of the booth.

SIDELINED

Early in my television sportscasting career I served as a rover, doing sideline analysis and the interviews with coaches and players on the field before and after the games. It's a job that they give mostly to former athletes and beautiful women today. There is some logic to that. Players and coaches aren't always in a talkative mood then, so it helps to have someone familiar (or gorgeous) to make them comfortable.

Sometimes the interview subjects are downright hostile, too. Norm Van Brocklin was named head coach of the terrible Atlanta Falcons three games into the 1968 season. Two weeks later the Falcons played the Giants, who were then quarterbacked by Fran Tarkenton, who had feuded publicly with Van Brocklin when both were with the Vikings. There was bad blood between the two, and my director—aware that I knew both men—wanted me to get the feud stirred up before the game.

I asked Van Brocklin if he'd be willing to let me "moderate" an interview with him and Tarkenton on the field.

"We don't have to dredge that up again, do we?" the coach asked.

I persisted, saying it would be a good way to clear the air and put their feud behind him.

"Okay. If Tarkenton will do it, then I'll do it," he said.

Next I asked Fran, a famous scrambler, and he signed on.

The Giants completed their pregame warm-ups first, and Fran joined us on the sideline, so I started the interview.

"Do you still have bad feelings for Norm?"

"No, no, no. That's all in the past. Norm was just trying to win ball-games when I played for him," he said.

We talked a few minutes, but Tarkenton, who was nobody's fool, would not be baited. He played the role of a United Nations peacemaker. So I thanked him and he returned to his team.

Then Van Brocklin walked up, but he wasn't looking nearly as serene as his former quarterback. He'd heard me asking loaded questions. Still, I teed it up: "Coach, you heard what Fran said about it being all in the past. Do you feel the same way?"

Van Brocklin clenched his fists, looked straight into the camera, and said, "I'm not gonna talk about that @%!&!"

End of interview.

PAIRED UP

I was always pushing to get up in the booth, to be part of the game broadcast team. But being the broadcast guy on the sidelines had its moments, and while I worked my way up I tried to make myself useful on the sidelines, too.

During a Giants game at Yankee stadium, the innovative director Tony Verna asked me to carry a Polaroid camera on the sidelines and shoot multiple photos of the wide receiver and other players in various phases of offensive formations. The idea was that I would take a sequence of photographs focusing on certain players, then return to the television truck and go over them to analyze what each guy was doing on each play. I spent the better part of the first half analyzing the sequences and then reporting my findings to the director, who relayed them to the team of announcers broadcasting the play-by-play and color analysis. It was very low-tech, but it was the beginning of the practice of "isolating" players on camera, which led to the earliest forms of the instant replay. Tony Verna was the mastermind, but I like to think I was in the trenches for those innovations.

Before too long, though, I worked my way up to the broadcast booth full-time. Initially I was teamed with a couple of legendary pros—Ray Scott and Jack Buck. They became role models for me, and it was a thrill to work alongside them. Ray, in particular, had great pipes, a real Cadillac of a voice. His commentary was Spartan, very understated, but also filled with dramatic tones. I picked up on his pared-down style and adopted it.

In his classic staccato style, Ray stabbed out the names and phrases: "Starr . . . Dowler . . . touchdown!" He was not a "happy talk" chatterbox. He did not try to overshadow the game with his personality, a lesson many modern sportscasters don't get.

Bill MacPhail, our CBS sports director, reinforced my inclination to keep it simple. "Just remember, Pat, I'll never criticize you for saying too little," he said.

Ray and I did many big Packers games as well as other premiere match-ups. We clicked, and soon we were the number-one TV team at CBS. Since Ray was a perfectionist and a stickler for preparation—always careful about getting players' names right—I worked on that, too.

I did my first color broadcast paired with Ray—although he wasn't in the booth and it wasn't actually a football game that I called. Ray had flown the red-eye from a game in Minnesota to San Francisco to cover a 49ers game in Kesar Stadium with me, and he was sick. At the end of the second quarter, he dashed to the bathroom, leaving me to cover the half-time performance, which the TV announcers did in those days. I knew it was a band—but that's all I knew, because Ray had all the notes on the performance with him in the men's room.

Just as I realized this, the director said to me, "Go." Well, I didn't know who the band was, where they were from, or what they were playing. So my comments consisted of, "Here comes the band . . . Don't they look good? . . . Isn't that pretty! . . . What a pageant! . . . Listen to that music." That was my whole play-by-play. Don't look for it on tape at the Broadcasting Hall of Fame.

Ray and I were in Kansas City covering the Chiefs and the Dallas Cowboys for another game. At that time, announcers usually did their own opening segments. When it came time to introduce the teams, we broadcast over the stadium's P.A. system. Then we introduced the performance of the national anthem. When the singer came out in Kansas City, Ray said to the TV audience and the game crowd: "And now, Ladies and Gentlemen, to sing the national anthem, Miss Marilyn Monroe!"

They cut the microphone off. I looked at my partner, who looked at me like there was nothing wrong. Ray didn't have a clue that he'd just resurrected a long-gone Hollywood icon.

"Ray, Marilyn Monroe has been dead for quite some time," I said.

He nodded but then asked a curious question: "What are we going to do?"

"I think we'd better correct *your* mistake," I said.

So he waited until the song was over, and then offered a correction, sort of: "Ladies and Gentlemen, that was Miss Marilyn *May*, from Kansas City."

BROADCAST BUCK

Unfortunately, Ray Scott got mad at CBS a few years later because he wasn't picked to do a Super Bowl broadcast, and he abruptly quit. I ended up getting paired with the more whimsical Jack Buck as the top-tier CBS sports team. Jack was a fun-loving, gregarious Irish guy with a more relaxed approach than any announcer I'd worked with. Yet he was also known as a great baseball broadcaster, so he was a very busy guy. Jack was smooth and professional, but very funny. More than anyone, Buck showed me that it was okay to have a good time in the booth. Every time we went to the coast we stopped in Las Vegas, going and coming. He liked to gamble, but mostly he liked being out and around people.

"This isn't Westminster Abbey, Pat. It's a diversion. Loosen up," he'd tell me.

Jack believed that if we were having fun, our audience would, too.

In 1970, just before Super Bowl IV in New Orleans featuring Kansas City against Minnesota, Jack and I were prepping when Jack Schneider, the distinguished boss at CBS, dropped in to give us a pep talk.

"We picked you two because we think you've done the best job during the season. You're our top guys," he told us. "Just do your normal good job."

Schneider started to leave the booth, then stopped and left us one parting thought: "Oh, and don't forget; there will be forty million people watching you!"

So much for relaxing and having fun.

MONDAY NIGHT FIGHT

Television and pro football were made for each other, and the NFL had long tinkered with the idea of moving one game off the weekend schedule and televising it during prime time on a weekday to snag even more TV viewers and ad dollars. The league floated the idea as early as 1964, but they'd pitched Friday as the game day, and that brought protests from high-school football fans who didn't want to have to choose between the kids and the pros.

NFL commissioner Pete Rozelle didn't give up. As an experiment, he scheduled the Packers to play the Lions on September 28, 1964, a Monday night. It wasn't televised, but it drew the largest crowd ever for a pro game in Detroit's Tiger Stadium. That got Rozelle pumped up about Monday night football. He scheduled one Monday night game for each season from 1966 to 1969. CBS broadcast the first two, and NBC did the second set. The games attracted big viewing audiences and a lot of good publicity, so Rozelle tried to get the CBS, NBC, and ABC to bid on exclusive broadcast rights for a weekly Monday night game.

I was there when Pete pitched his idea to network sports director Bill MacPhail and CBS president Bob Wood. Pete had invited us for a lunch cruise aboard the *Triple Eagle*, up the Hudson past the George Washington Bridge toward Willet's Point. It was a beautiful day, but a bad one for CBS sports.

For the main course, Pete served up *Monday Night Football* on a silver platter to the CBS executives. "I really don't want anyone else involved. I want CBS to have it because of your network's loyalty to the NFL over the years," he said.

Rozelle all but begged Bill Wood to take the concept and run with it. Everyone agreed that it was sure to be a big hit in the ratings. Wood listened intently, and then asked for a telephone. From aboard the yacht he called Chairman Bill Paley to pitch him on this golden opportunity.

Paley shot him down.

"I think we're doing pretty well with our Monday night shows," Paley said. "We've got *Gunsmoke, Here's Lucy,* then Doris Day and Carol Burnett. It's a pretty solid lineup. I'd hate to upset that balance."

I wanted to jump overboard. I didn't need another workday, but the Monday night game looked like a sure winner to me. I was shocked when NBC turned it down, too. Rozelle had no option but to offer it to struggling ABC, the third wheel in television broadcasting, which wasn't even doing pro football at the time.

They only stuck with it for thirty-six years—and reaped rewards that were the envy of the other networks. *Monday Night Football* rejuvenated ABC and brought millions of new fans into the fold for the NFL. The Monday night broadcasts became "must-see TV," in no little part thanks to the many "colorful" personalities who sat in the ABC booth, including the original team that featured my commuting pal Howard Cosell, Keith Jackson, and "Dandy" Don Meredith.

BUCK PASSING

I was disappointed that CBS didn't grab the *Monday Night Football* franchise, but the network did its best to keep me busy. One morning during the football season the new CBS sports president Bob Wussler, called me at home in New Jersey, where he had moved, and asked, "What are you doing?"

I told him I was just relaxing.

"Can you make it into New York for lunch?"

When the boss calls, you come running. Over lunch, Wussler dropped a bomb.

"I got problems with you and Jack Buck," he said.

My initial reaction was to be defensive. We'd been the number-one team for quite a while at that point, I noted.

"You are the number-one team. You are the best. My problem is, I can't tell which one of you is talking at any given time," Wussler said. "You sound too much alike."

I had to admit he had a point. Later in his career, Jack's voice got gravelly from smoking, but we did have similar baritones. Still, I wasn't enthused about shaking up our winning team. Of course, Wussler was the boss, so I really didn't have a vote in the matter. He let me know it was going to happen, so I took the opportunity to make a pitch.

"As long as I'm going to make a change, I'd like to try doing play-by-play," I said.

To my surprise, Wussler was willing to give it a try. And he wasn't even going to make me do a try-out.

"If you're gonna do it, let's do it this week," he said.

"In the middle of the season?" I replied.

He told me I'd worked with enough great play-by-play guys that I should have absorbed all I needed to know.

"Whom do you want to work with?" he asked. Wussler was full of surprises that day.

This time it was my turn. I had been doing voice-overs for NFL Films in Philadelphia and for the *This Week in the NFL* highlight show. Another NFL player-turned-announcer was working with me on the project—my former Eagles nemesis, Tom Brookshier.

I suggested that Brookie would be a good match for me because our voices were distinctly different. Brookshier still lived in the "City of Brotherly Love." He had taken over *This Week in the NFL* after announcer Charlie Jones experienced some trouble balancing his New York commitments and social life with the out-of-town obligations of the show.

Wussler liked the idea of Brookshier as my booth mate. He called Brookie and sealed the deal. This new pairing came together so fast that I had some second thoughts. Brookshier and I had been getting along well doing the highlight show, but we had a less amicable history as players. In 1959, after I caught a short pass in the final minutes of a lopsided win over Philadelphia, he belted me so hard in the head that my helmet split open. We both hit the ground, and as I was trying to recover my senses I lashed out at him for the shot to the head.

"What's wrong with you?"

"You shouldn't even be playing! You got the game won," he said.

It was not an auspicious start to our relationship. Still, we hadn't butted heads since. After our first meeting, we were generally more cordial to each other when we'd meet at parties and events. But working together in the high-stress broadcast booth was going to be a test of our mutual civility.

I didn't have long to worry about it. With only three days of preparation we did the Cardinals-Giants game together that weekend. There was not a hitch. We actually had good chemistry, and before we knew it we were having fun.

The play-by-play role also came easily to me. All those years of working alongside the best in the business paid off. It wasn't long before Brookie and I had established ourselves as the number-one football broadcast team at CBS and, soon, the number-one all-sports broadcast team at CBS. It's served me right, I guess. In high school and college, I was the kid who wanted to be involved in every possible sport. CBS was making my wishes come true. Soon they had me broadcasting not only NFL games but NBA games, too, not to mention horse shows, figure skating, ice shows, and even the Westminster Dog Show. What I knew about show dogs you could fit in a doggie bag, but luckily they teamed me with Roger Karas, "the voice of Westminster," who knew every breed and which way its tail twitched. I did the lead-ins for commercials and tried to stay out of his way.

HOLLYWOOD CALLS

Brookie didn't get called in for dog detail, but he did join me in my Silver Screen debut. Since we were the top football broadcasting team on television, Brookie and I were cast as—this was a real stretch—ourselves in *Black Sunday,* director John Frankenheimer's 1977 movie about a terrorist attack at the Super Bowl.

The movie film crew shot a lot of footage for the movie during Super Bowl X in Miami in January 1976. While Brookie and I worked the real game, they taped game scenes, crowd shots, and shots of us in the booth at the Orange Bowl. After Pittsburgh slipped by Dallas 21–17 to win the title championship, we flew to Hollywood, where Frankenheimer had built an exact replica of the Orange Bowl broadcast booth in a rented warehouse.

The next day we had lunch with one of the lead actors, Bruce Dern, in Frankenheimer's office. Dern had a reputation as a rebel, and he and the director spent most of the meal arguing over the actor's costume choice. Dern didn't want to wear a coat and tie to play a disillusioned blimp pilot who was the pawn of terrorists. The two argued about it, and eventually Frankenheimer won that battle. We wondered if the intense actor might turn into a real terrorist after that. I think they were careful to keep live ammunition out of his hands.

When it was time to roll the cameras, Brookie and I sat in the replica booth and watched a tape of Super Bowl X, describing what we saw just like the real game. Unbeknownst to us, Frankenheimer had planted a guy with a machine gun behind a screen. With the cameras going, the "terrorist" jumped out of nowhere and started blasting his machine gun. If the director was looking for cinema verité, he got it. It scared the hell out of us, and we reacted just as he'd hoped.

"What the @%!& was that?" Brookie shouted.

"I don't know, but let's get out of here!" I said.

As we scrambled out of the booth, Frankenheimer came onto the set applauding.

"That was great! Just great!" he said. "That's the reaction I wanted! I can't use it, but it was terrific!"

The expletive was a genuine gut reaction from Brookie, but it was a little too real for the director to use. We tried the scene again, though the second time we knew what was coming and didn't react as realistically. Still, it was good enough for Hollywood. The movie was a box-office and critical success.

Brookie and I are still waiting for our Oscars from the Academy.

HORSEPLAY

Back in the real world, the two of us were living like we hadn't a care in the world—or wives or families. It was a very seductive and hedonistic lifestyle that eventually took a toll on both of us. But we were swept up in Boys' Land. We had a lot of money and a lot of down time, and we were usually traveling away from wives and family responsibilities. We had our dream jobs, and we were determined to enjoy the fruit until we'd squeezed out every last drop of juice.

Our work schedules were like one mad dash from game to game, city to city. We even became adept at drinking while dashing. On one memorable weekend, we did an NFL game in Washington on Saturday, then jumped in a van for a four-hour drive to Philadelphia for another game on Sunday. Fearing that we could become parched in the desert between Washington and Philadelphia, we stocked the van with Jack Daniels and Scotch. We still considered ourselves professional athletes, the sport being competitive drinking. It seemed like a clever concept at the time.

Our faithful spotter, Lance Barrow, was the designated driver for the trip, which quickly became a drinking contest on wheels. Our director, Sandy Grossman, and producer, Chuck Milton, were on the Scotch team. Brookie and I proudly represented the Jack Daniels squad. When the wheels hit the road, we hit the bottle. You could practically hear the brain cells being destroyed as we drank down the road. No one seemed concerned about the fact that we were scheduled to do an interview with some of the Eagles when we got there.

By the time we approached the outer limits of Philadelphia, we had gone way past the outer limits of sobriety. I can only assume that we'd also lost the ability to reason. That's my only explanation for what happened next.

"I've got an idea," Brookie said ominously. "Why don't you guys tie me on the front of the van like we've been deer hunting? You know, pretend you shot me and slung me over the hood?"

It was not unusual for Brookie to think like this, even when sober. It was strange, however, that the rest of us thought it sounded like a hilarious idea. And so, we pulled into the Eagles' camp with my partner strapped across the hood.

The players, who were preparing for a big game, were not amused. "Why should we talk to these guys?" I heard one of them say. "They aren't going to remember anything."

I don't recall who won the drinking contest, but Brookie and I didn't win over many of the Eagles during that trip. We didn't care. We thought we were bulletproof. Every night was boys' night out when we were on the road—and sometimes when we were home, too.

After broadcasting a Rams game in Los Angeles on a Sunday, we flew back to New York in the wee hours of Monday morning. We swilled Jack Daniels on the flight back, and we wanted to continue the party on the ground. We arranged to meet golf commentator Ben Wright at a Manhattan steakhouse rather than go to our homes. We raised such a ruckus that management asked us to take the party somewhere else. We stumbled out on to Second Avenue. When we couldn't flag down a cab, Brookie decided to lie down in the middle of the street.

"That'll stop a cab," he said.

Taxi drivers wisely steered clear. But a horse-drawn carriage did come clomping up. The carriage master was an Irishman who seemed to have some familiarity with soused parties on the streets of Manhattan. We asked for a ride to the Plaza Hotel. I climbed in the back seat with the other members of our traveling circus, but Brookie wanted to ride shotgun. He'd seen too many cowboy movies with runaway stagecoaches, I guess. He sat next to the Irish driver and shared limericks. As we headed up Sixth Avenue, Brookie rose and looked back at us, maybe thinking some bandits were coming.

Standing up in a moving horse carriage with alcohol-impaired motor skills was not a good idea. Brookie went down with the first bump in the road. He fell out of the carriage into the middle of Sixth Avenue, landing on his noggin right in front of the CBS building. The symbolism escaped us at the time.

"He's fine," I diagnosed. "He landed on his head."

He did appear to be okay, though at that point, no one in the vicinity was qualified to judge. We arrived at the Plaza somewhat worse for the wear. As we paid the driver a handsome tip, the Irishman expressed sorrow that he couldn't join us for the rest of the party.

"Ya' fellas seem to be havin' quite a time," he said. "And I'd sure like to go wit' ya'—if I could." He wasn't serious, but that fact was lost on us.

"Come on then, go with us, we'll have a whiskey upstairs," I said.

"What am I gonna do with me horse?"

"Bring the horse," I said.

No animals were injured in the making of this fiasco, thanks largely to hotel security. We had unhitched the innocent horse and removed his oat bag in case he wanted to snack in the elevator. We'd even escorted our noble steed up the steps to the hotel's rear entrance. But the horse spooked at the sliding glass door. (It must have preferred less expensive hotels.) When the horse reared up and whinnied, hotel security came running to the rescue. We had reservations. The horse didn't.

Our shenanigans that night and on many others managed to offend a good portion of the New York social scene over the years. We were even banned from the grand King Cole Bar in the St. Regis Hotel. The bar is named for a mural depicting Old King Cole, created by the noted illustrator Maxfield Parrish. Brookie and I were drinking with a couple of friends, listening to the piano at the round bar and exchanging witty repartee about the mural—as I recall we were making juvenile jokes about how all the king's horses and all the king's men were recoiling from what must have been a massive gas attack unleashed by King Cole.

Brookie and I were wound up.

"Patrick!" he said.

I knew that when he called me that, trouble was imminent. Brookie next made a disparaging comment to me about the pianist, noting that he appeared to be wearing a particularly bad toupee. I sensed danger. But before I could rein in my broadcasting partner, Brookie was off to the races.

He scampered around the bar, dove over the top of the piano, and snatched the toupee off the pianist's head. Then, to my dismay, he brought it back to me like a retriever with a stick. I swear his tail was wagging. "See, I told you so!" he said, brandishing his prize.

Bedlam hit the bar. Other patrons were either questioning the legitimacy of our births or laughing hysterically.

The bar manager was not among the amused. He took me aside and said quietly, "Look, you seem like the saner of the two. You don't owe me anything, but would you make me a promise?"

I nodded and took one last look at King Cole, since I knew what was coming.

"Will you promise me you will leave our establishment and never come back?"

I whistled to my not-so-golden retriever and we hightailed it out of that prestigious watering hole. When we reached the corner of Madison Avenue and Fifty-second, I realized Brookie was not with me. I turned to see him scurrying up behind, still holding the pianist's hairpiece. Brookie had collected his scalp for the evening.

Although our celebrity status and lucrative jobs got us into the finest places, the antics of our extended childhoods ensured that we were frequently asked to leave in short order. When we did get to hang around, though, we met some interesting people. One night, Brookshier and I attended a CBS dinner in honor of the team of *NFL Today*, Jimmy "The Greek" Snyder and Brent Musburger. The event, which was held before Jimmy the Greek punched Musburger in a Manhattan bar, was at the posh 21 Club in New York's Theatre District.

We were at the club's watering hole, doing our best to deplete the vodka supply prior to the festivities, when Brookie tapped me on the shoulder. "Pat, look over there. It's a guy in a Nixon mask. He's acting like he wants to talk to us."

I looked over and saw a man motioning to us. Then I realized it wasn't a mask. It was Richard Nixon, and he sent a Secret Service agent over to tell us he wanted to chat. I'd heard Nixon was a sports fan, and that he knew his stuff. He was also very flattering of our work. He even called us "great Americans."

I was very grateful that Brookie didn't bring up Watergate or the impeachment process. He behaved, and we had a long discussion about football with the disgraced former president who was quite cordial. Nixon was crazy about football and anxious to get our take on what was going on behind the scenes in the NFL. We had a long discussion, which made us late for dinner, but we had a good excuse: "Sorry, we were out in the bar yakking with the former leader of the free world," Brookie announced as we sat down. The next day, couriers arrived at both our homes with personally autographed copies of *RN: The Memoirs of Richard Nixon.*

FALL FROM GRACE

There were lessons to be learned about the abuse of power and privilege in the Nixon memoir, but they escaped me at the time. In fact, I still recall my days on the road with Brookie as one of the most enjoyable periods of my life. We painted every town red, and we had so much fun doing our jobs that the fans could feel it, too. People would write and say they'd sit down as a family and watch a football game and feel like we were a part of their gathering. In seven-and-a-half years as the number-one announcing team, we did three Super Bowls—X, XII, and XIV—and hundreds of other sports broadcasts.

The rest of the world was caught up in the Bicentennial, the red dye scare, the dawn of Apple computers, the Son of Sam killer, and the Jonestown Massacre; we were focused on the next broadcast and how many drinks it would take to get us there and back. We didn't pay much attention to anyone or anything else, including our wives and our families. We were a great broadcasting team and we truly loved our work and the excitement of our lives, but we effectively shut out the world around us. It got to the point that we never wanted to go home.

When we did return, we spent as little time at home as possible. We did most of our broadcast work on the weekends, but we usually hit the road on Wednesdays and often didn't come home until Tuesday. We didn't have home lives. When we were there, we chafed at the expectations and responsibilities. We had become addicted to the celebrity lifestyle we led on the road. The drinking and the partying got to be a habitual thing. Brookie and I had a lot of friends in common, and we were invited to many events. We were the life of most of them, but we often paid for it with tough mornings.

Neither of us thought our work suffered from all of the partying, but I'm sure it must have been affected in ways we did not discern. News of our exploits often filtered back to the CBS brass in New York. At first they were amused, but eventually they became concerned that we were either going to embarrass the network or kill ourselves.

"One of them is going to show up dead some morning," a CBS executive predicted. "They can't go on like this."

CHAPTER SEVEN

MADDEN 'N' ME

BROOKIE HAD TO TAKE A BREAK FROM THE BOOTH IN THE FALL OF 1980 to introduce his daughter Betsy at a debutante ball in Philadelphia. To replace him, CBS brought in John Madden, a highly qualified temp if there ever was one. John had recently left coaching to try sportscasting. John was waiting for me when I arrived at the broadcast booth at the stadium in Tampa. We only had a few minutes to get reacquainted before the pregame taping began, so neither one of us knew what to expect of our first broadcast together.

I had met John several times during his successful coaching career with the Oakland Raiders, but I really didn't know him personally. I did know that he had 103 wins and only thirty-two losses in his ten seasons as coach there. He'd also won Super Bowl XI in January of 1977 against the Minnesota Vikings. His overall win percentage, including playoff victories, was second only to Vince Lombardi's at Green Bay. So I figured John had to know the game as well as about anybody else CBS could find. Yet I worried that he might have a tough time being thrown into the fire so quickly—and I wondered if I'd get burned, too.

Tampa's stadium, which seated more than a hundred thousand people, was dubbed "the Big Sombrero" by ESPN sportscaster Chris

Berman because of its broad, hat-like shape. The broadcasting facilities were unusually high up into the stands, and it was quite a hike getting to them. When I reached the lofty booth, Madden was there. He wore a coat and tie, a departure from his coaching days, when he was known to favor shirtsleeves even in freezing weather.

As we settled in, John was obviously uncomfortable. His jacket was soaked with sweat. I wrote it off to the Florida heat and humidity at first. But John became even more ill at ease as we stepped onto a little over-hang that jutted out from the rear of the booth, providing a nice back-drop of the city for our pregame show. Sweat droplets ran down his face and he was flushed. I worried that he might be having a heart attack. If not, he certainly didn't appear ready for prime time.

It was my turn to panic. The new guy wasn't going to make it through the broadcast at this rate. Still, there was nothing I could do about it. We had to roll. John got through the opening of our pregame segment all right, but the sweat was still just rolling off of him. When we'd finished taping the pregame, we walked back inside the booth. There, he confided to me that it wasn't pregame jitters affecting him.

"Pat, I'm afraid I just can't stand heights," he confessed.

I told the producer that we wouldn't be doing anymore scenic back-ground shots with our backs to the open air. Once we returned to the booth, John relaxed. We then went over our approach to the broadcast, including what each of us would focus on. John was a little nervous in the first few minutes of the broadcast, but by the end of the first quarter, I was getting a sense that he was something special.

GOOD MATCH

John knew many nuances of the game, both on offense and defense. Not only was his insight keen, his enthusiasm was genuine. For two guys

(Top Left) My cousin Mary Lou and my grandmother, Augusta Georgia Summerall, who I was probably coaxing to play catch.

(Top Right) My throwing form here demonstrates why I became a kicker early in my playing career and why my grandmother stayed in her chair.

(Left) I was a master of the set shot as a Columbia High Tiger in Lake City perhaps because those tight shorts prevented doing much else.

(Top) We were Florida state high school basketball champs in 1947 and my teammates Jerry Willis and Winton Criswell (left to right) were big reasons.

(Above) "The Kick" that split the uprights against all odds and to Vince Lombardi's amazement in our N.Y. Giants game against the Cleveland Browns at Yankee Stadium in 1958.

(Top) My Giants teammates
Frank Gifford, left, and Bob
Schnelker were thinking of having
my kicking foot bronzed after the
Browns game in 1958.

(Left) Can you tell I still get a kick
out of this record-breaking boot?
Check out that follow through!

(Right) My daughter Susie learned to punt at an early age.

(Above) On my first day as a CBS announcer, I had to overcome microphone awe.

(Above) Susie and my son Jay help me tee it up in the park across from the Concourse Plaza Hotel in the Bronx.

(Left) Proof that my hair did not turn gray before 1964.

(Above) I wrangled some time with my shy former Yankee Stadium locker mate for my first interview during their spring training camp.

(Top) I may have had the only rented tuxedo in this crowd that included from left, my CBS boss Bill MacPhail, Jets owner Leon Hess and Giants owner Wellington Mara.

(Center) Frank Gifford, Bill MacPhail, Kansas City Chiefs owner Lamar Hunt, and CBS salesman Kenny Flower joined me for this glamour shot.

(Bottom) Not to be mistaken for choir boys, me and my sideburns are flanked by Frank Gifford and my road roommate and holder Charlie Conerly.

(Top) I was just another pretty face on the podium with Jack Buck and Hank Stram.

(Center) NFL Commissioner Pete Rozelle patiently waited for me to tell him something he didn't know.

(Bottom) Giants coach Jim Lee Howell and broadcasting giant Chris Schenkel give me some tips on pre-game preparation.

(Right) The kids say goodbye as I leave our home in Connecticut for another road trip.

(Above) Brookie and I share a "rare" moment of levity. This photo so typified our partnership that we used it as a Christmas card.

(Top) This promo shot for NFL Films had Brookie and me lost in a sea of helmet heads.

(Center) As a boy, sports were my all-consuming passion and as an adult I was blessed to live the dream as this CBS publicity shot shows.

(Bottom) John Madden, who does not like heights, was probably hoping I wouldn't let him fall backwards in this photo taken before we teamed up to broadcast the highest rated Super Bowl of all time, Super Bowl XVI in Detroit.

(Top Left) At Pebble Beach with Ken Venturi and the man in the beret Phil Harris, who kept us in stitches while his designated "pourer" kept Phil from getting parched.

(Top Right) Tennis anyone? I'm regaling Tony Trabert and John Newcombe about my high school hitchhike to the state tennis finals before we broadcast the French Open at Roland Garos stadium in Paris.

(Above) From the look on my face, my producer must have just told me that someone ate all the roast beef sandwiches on the pre-game lunch table.

(Top) Our director Frank Chirkinian tries to explain to our NBA crew—me, Hot Rod Hundley and analyst Elgin Baylor—that there is no "booth" in basketball.

(Center) It took years of training but I finally got Madden to gesticulate with the outside arm, so I didn't have to duck or flinch so much.

(Bottom) The stands may be empty but John Madden and I are just getting warmed up.

(Top Left) Cheri is surrounded by two well-dressed turkeys prior to our crew's pre-game Thanksgiving dinner.

(Top Right) Mickey Mantle and Greer Johnson joined Cheri and me at the Masters Tournament in Augusta.

(Right) Former President Gerald Ford invited me to play with him and NBA coach Chuck Daley at Ford's annual golf tournament in Vail.

(Bottom) Family wedding picture March 16, 1996

(Left) We may look like tourists fresh off the bus but this is "The Team" prepped for the Super Bowl in Miami. That's Madden, Bob Stenner, Sandy Grossman, and me.

(Center Left) Cheri and I were delighted that John and Virginia Madden came from California to our wedding in the Madden Cruiser, which definitely livened up the church parking lot.

(Center Right) Tom Landry hosted his own golf tournament and he invited me to make sure the rough got good coverage.

(Above) My final Masters broadcast in 1994, with a motley crew that included Peter Kostis, Ben Wright, Gary McCord, Jim Nantz, Ken Venturi, Frank Chirkinian, the good guy in white (pants) and Tom Weiskopf

(Right) This shot with my lovely Cheri always makes me wonder why I spent so much of my life side by side with other men talking sports.

(Top Right) I often told Betty Ford that I preferred her golf tournament to her clinic, but I was grateful for both.

(Right) NFL commander in chief Paul Tagliabue brought former U.S. Commander in Chief Jimmy Carter up to the booth though the Secret Service wasn't so sure he'd be safe up there with us.

(Above) My kids and grandkids, minus one who had yet to arrive.

(Top) Augusta National's Jack Stephens gave me my first coat when I played at Arkansas but I could never get him to give me one of those green jackets.

(Center) I know mine is just silver hair but I swear that Billy Graham's is a halo.

(Bottom) I was in good company—Tom Landry, former President Gerald Ford and Roosevelt Grier—when I received the Leukemia Foundation's Ernie Davis Award given in memory of the late Heisman Trophy winner who exemplified "excellence of character and integrity, and service to mankind."

(Top) Now this team has game. It is my Jacksonville Mayo Clinic transplant team huddled together at the 2005 Super Bowl with (left to right) Dr. Hewitt, Dr. Yip, Dr. Willingham, Dr. Steers, the patient, Dr. Kramer, Dr. Mai, Dr. Hughes, and seated, Lorrie Yell, Vicky Topcik, Dr. Harnois, and Lora Brown.

(Right) Adron Shelby, "a special angel," was my transplant donor and I will always honor his gift.

Adron DeMarkis Shelby
1990—2004

who had never worked together, we fell into a natural rhythm very quickly. With other temporary partners, I had often resorted to hand signals to let them know when I was done speaking, but it wasn't necessary in John's case. We were in sync.

It also helped that John liked to stand up during the game, just like me. I switched to standing during broadcasts when I went from the analyst slot to play-by-play. As an analyst, I was focusing on certain players and had a sense of where my line of sight needed to be for each play. But in doing play-by-play, I felt I could get a better sense of the action if I stood. I would watch the monitor until the huddle broke, and then I would turn toward the field to watch the play develop.

I knew play-by-play announcers who stayed fixed on the monitor, regardless of what was happening. I've actually heard other play-by-play people say, "We don't really need to be at the stadium. We can just do it off the television monitor." I think that's bull. When I watch the live action, I pick up on the little things that are vital to the game and have a better feel for what is happening on the field.

For the same reason, I never worked a game with the windows closed in the broadcasting booth, regardless of the weather. John and I were also in accord on that. We wanted to experience the elements because that's a big part of the game. When Brookie returned the following week, I learned that the network bosses had decided to break up our team. The decision was made mostly because of our off-camera carousing. They'd decided to split us up before we got into trouble or before we let our social lives affect our performances. Brookie and I went out in style by going—just as spectators—to Super Bowl XV, on January 25, 1981, in New Orleans. It was a great game in which the Raiders, led by a rejuvenated Jim Plunkett, upset the Eagles.

We had quite a time. Our hotel suite became party central. It seemed like everyone who came to town for the game passed through our room—and some of them stayed. The party went on for the whole week, before, during, and after the game. Our guests—invited and otherwise—had a good time, judging from the final tab. When we went to check out, I got the car while Brookie went down to settle the bill. By the time I got to the lobby, the printout of the bill from our party room stretched all the way across the lobby. Brookie was just standing there, pondering it.

"This looks like the Magna Carta," he finally said.

It was tough to break up what had been a great partnership. I think we were both aware that we'd had too much of a good thing for a long while. We were a good team on the air, and too good when we were on the prowl. Yet, even after we no longer worked together, we remained the closest of friends. It was a good thing for me that our friendship held up. Brookie, who left broadcasting a short time later, was a great guy to work with and to hang out with, but he proved to be an even better, caring friend.

After my final game with Brookie, I was briefly paired with another former coach, Hank Stram. He was a great broadcaster, but my earlier collaboration with Madden had triggered a great deal of enthusiasm back at CBS headquarters in Manhattan. When the fall of 1981 rolled around and a new NFL season began, CBS designated Madden and me as the top-tier broadcast team.

MADDEN MASTERY

There are many knowledgeable coaches, ex-coaches, and other great football analysts, but few of them have the ability to condense their wisdom into ten-to-fifteen-second sound bites. That's how much time we typically had to get a word in between plays during an NFL game. Not only did we have to be concise, we also had to make sense. John Madden quickly became a master game analyst. He had the knowledge and the ability to communicate it quickly and clearly.

John came to broadcasting as a widely respected coach in the NFL ranks. He was an innovator as a coach, and he has been an innovator as a broadcaster. Before John came along, most announcers looked at maybe one game film during their preparation, and that was usually just a highlight film or a TV tape of the last game. Through his coaching connections, John could get special coaches' tapes that allowed you to watch the movements of all twenty-two players at the same time. John would stop and rewind the tapes repeatedly, looking for little things that made a difference, such as a tackle stepping back with the wrong foot or a guard giving up too much ground too quickly. Then he'd find a way to incorporate this information into the broadcast at an opportune time.

Before John became a broadcaster, none of us looked at the coaches' films like they do now. Because John remained such an astute student of the game, NFL head coaches often sought him out to get his take on things, and they still do. Mike Martz and Dick Vermeil are among the many who aren't afraid to tap his great football mind.

While John is respected throughout the league, he was not afraid to ask coaches sensitive questions, or to say things that might provoke them. During a telecast at Texas Stadium, John sided with a controversial call that went against Landry's Dallas Cowboys. After the game, I went to the suite of the Cowboys' general manager, Texas Schramm, with whom I'd enjoyed a long association and friendship. Before his thirty-year stint with the Cowboys began, Tex was assistant director of sports at CBS. He signed off on my hiring as the host of that Giants report, which I did for WCBS radio when I was still a player.

By the time I got to his suite, Tex had downed a couple of Jack Daniels. When I walked in, he glanced up but didn't say hello. I waited. A few seconds later, he launched into a tirade: "You tell that Madden guy that before he goes on the air and starts talking about things, he better learn the real truth about the rules. He doesn't know the rules. You tell him that."

"Tex, he's still in the booth," I said. "If you want to, you can go tell him yourself."

He didn't.

Tex Schramm may know more about football than 99.99 percent of the human race, but I never would bet against Madden. The more I worked with John in those early days, the more I realized that he was a unique talent with the potential to be without peer in our business. Not only was he an exceptionally bright guy, he worked harder at the homework than anybody I'd ever met. His enthusiastic attitude was infectious. I'd sit with him and watch game tapes for hours. Often, those little things he noticed impacted games in a big way.

Because I did not talk as much as many play-by-play guys, he had a little more latitude to make colorful and sometimes off-beat observations that added to our broadcasts. He took that ball and ran with it as his confidence grew. Soon, my partner in the booth was a one-man sound-effects machine, issuing booms and bams and whaps and doinks that became his trademark. Our television viewers didn't get to see that his sound effects were accompanied by sweeping hand gestures, which I had to learn to dodge to avoid being clothes-lined in the broadcast booth.

John's rabid interest in all aspects of football extended to the players, their personalities, and their personal lives. He was always up for wading into a locker room or a practice field to talk to the players and dig up anecdotes and information prior to a game. Sometimes we would learn about things that we couldn't repeat. Once we talked with a nose tackle who had just gotten out of jail on drug charges and had been a well-known steroid user. It was in the early 1990s, and Lyle Alzado had just died at the age of forty-three from an illness attributed to longtime steroid use. Alarmed, the NFL started cracking down on steroids. So when this nose tackle started naming suspected steroid users in the league, we weren't sure we wanted to hear it. But we couldn't help but laugh to ourselves when he said, "We're gonna see how tough and big they really are now that they can't use that artificial insemination anymore."

I turned to John and said, "I don't think we can use that on the air."

Though he has a wealth of knowledge and great technical skills that serve him well in his broadcast work, the thing that really made John and me a great team is that we shared a love of the game. Listening to him is like sitting next to the world's greatest football fan. Even in the booth, you could see him go tense and shut his eyes when a player on the field was about to take a big hit. John didn't just see it and talk about it, he felt it—and he helped our viewers feel it, too.

Although our personalities are very different, we rapidly became great friends. The only real split we ever had was over hardware. John became a pitchman for the Ace Hardware chain of stores while I represented the competing True Value Hardware chain. Those jobs gave us more than enough walking-around money.

We did have one other rather expensive split decision. When a small computer game software company approached us in 1988 about doing voice-overs for a new NFL computer game, John took his payments in stock, while I signed a four-year contract for $75,000 a year. I could have taken the stock, but I wasn't sure the company, Electronic Arts Sports, would be around very long.

I went for the cash, saying to myself, *I can't imagine this is gonna work.* I wanted to make certain I got paid because doing voice-overs for video games is mind-numbing work. I worked on the *Madden NFL Football* series with John for several years. We did our recordings separately for these game soundtracks, and the editors spliced our comments together to make it seem like we were standing side by side.

The challenge in doing voice-overs is to not go insane at the sound of your own voice. In the recording studio, you have to cover every possible play scenario. That takes about five solid days of work. For every team, you have to do a couple of their running backs and a couple of their top receivers. For example, with Jacksonville, you'd have to say:

"Fred Taylor for one."

"Fred Taylor for two."

"Fred Taylor for three."

And then you'd start all over for the lost yardage plays:

"Fred Taylor loses one."

"Fred Taylor loses two."

There are all kinds of throwing-and-catching scenarios, as well as kicking-and-punting scenarios, and dozens of different inflections to splice in. Sometimes, you get lost in the repetition, forget where you are, and have to start the recording drudgery all over again.

But John's decision to take the stock resulted in it being a little more worthwhile for him. I got a nice payment, but it was a flat sum paid over a four-year contract. The last time I asked him, his stock was worth millions more. The game became the most popular in history, bringing in more than $2 billion in sales, according to Electronic Arts.

I'd like to have a do-over on my EA Sports stock call.

The disparity in our video game paydays never caused a problem for John and me. Our bond was built around our shared love of the game. He sensed that, and often told me, "You're a football guy and I'm a football guy." John played at California Polytechnic State University and was drafted by the Eagles, although he suffered a serious knee injury in training camp and never got to play pro ball. But as a coach, he roamed the sidelines of many of the same decrepit fields I had played on. We knew the same football places and people.

There's no experience in broadcasting school that can take the place of being down on the field as a player or coach, knowing how deep the emotions run and what sacrifices you have to make to get an edge on game day. Sometimes I'd go down on the field before a game and just listen to warm-up drills. I'd hear players banging against one another and grunting, and I'd think, *My God! I once did that for a living? I did that for ten years?*

Often, as I was preparing to make a trip down to the field, I'd ask John if there was anything he wanted me to find out for him. Something might come up about the wind or the field or the type of shoes the players were wearing, and I knew it might be useful to him in the booth. Once, I spent a lot of time talking to 49ers coach Bill Walsh down on the field before a game. When I got back upstairs, an anxious John asked, "Well, what were you and Walsh talking about that whole time?" I said, "We were discussing a stock he thought I should invest in." John responded, "And here I thought you were getting the whole game plan."

FREE MADDEN

For all of his genius, John will be the first to admit that he has a few idiosyncrasies, which made him all the more interesting to work with. The big man cannot abide crowds. If he gets to feeling crowded in a restaurant or any other place, he is liable to just get up and leave. He cannot tolerate feeling constrained. Even tight shoelaces bother him, so generally he lets them flop freely.

His fear of air travel is well-known. During his coaching career, he flew with the team only out of necessity. He swore off this mode of transporation after having a panic attack on a flight out of Tampa in 1979. He told me that his dislike of airplanes comes more from the fear of being confined or "encased," as he put it, than from fear of turbulence or a plane crash. (John feels the same way about elevators. He would rather walk ten flights of stairs than get in a confined space that he can't exit at will.)

For a long time after he swore off air travel, John mostly relied on Amtrak for his cross-country trips. But he eventually got fed up with trains, their unreliable schedules, and their limited points of departure and arrival. And so, the Madden Cruiser was born. The first version was an old customized Greyhound bus that rolled out in 1987. It became so famous that sponsors signed on, and the Madden Cruiser was upgraded to a first-class motor coach. But even this didn't completely cure John's claustrophobia. I'd often ride with him from the hotel to the stadiums, and even on such short hauls it wasn't uncommon for him to have his bus drivers pull off the side of the road so he could get out for a while.

It is interesting that John, who was so engaging and talkative on the air, is a bit of a loner in his personal life. John can be a great dinner companion because he is interested and knowledgeable in a wide range of things, but he isn't gregarious by nature. He is more inclined to stay home and read than to hit the nightspots.

A gentle guy and a devoted family man, John would always ask about my family. When the mother of our agent died, he showed up at the funeral without fanfare. He wasn't one to talk about his feelings, but often he surprises people with his concern for them.

I worked with John for two decades, but faith doesn't come up much in sportscasting. So I grew concerned when John was at our house one night for a network crew party. The Cowboys' chaplain, my good friend John Weber, was there along with about fifty other folks. So, before we sat down to eat, I announced that I wanted John to lead us in prayer.

A look of fear crossed John Madden's face, and I realized that he thought I was calling on him to do the prayer. So I said, "Not you, John. I meant John Weber."

A look of relief swept over him. When I apologized later for scaring him, he said, "Oh, no. I had one ready, Pat. I had one in the can."

I asked him what prayer he had called to mind on such short notice.

"It was 'Now I Lay Me Down to Sleep,'" he said.

THE A-TEAM

My association with John was much more subdued and less social than the one I had with his predecessor. Still, we had our exciting moments. At the end of our first season, we got the call to do Super Bowl XVI, pitting Joe Montana's San Francisco 49ers against the Cincinnati Bengals in the Silverdome in Pontiac, Michigan.

It was an exciting day for both of us, but we ran into a few hitches. John and I were doing the opening segment before the game, sitting on a bench outside the booth with our backs to the field, holding hand-microphones instead of wearing headsets. I asked John the last question for our segment, and while the camera remained on him during his response, I hustled off the set to don my headset for the game broadcast.

But I could not find my headset. John chattered away while I hunted for it. There's an axiom in broadcasting that if you can't find a piece of equipment, you follow the cable. I started pulling on the cable, but stopped when I realized it ran right underneath John. He was talking to one hundred million viewers with my headset lodged firmly under his ample behind. John saw me, and I'm sure he was wondering why I was just standing there, staring at him. He had no earpiece, so no one could tell him that he was sitting on my headset.

The CBS production crew started pointing at his rear end, but John didn't have a clue what they were trying to tell him. Finally, he finished his bit and stood up, and my headset came springing out. If John were to describe it, he'd probably say, "Sproing!" It was a bit bent out of shape, but I straightened it out in a hurry. I still had the coin-toss to call out in the middle of the field with a national audience looking on. Fortunately, the headset worked, though I tried not to think about how it had gotten so warm.

The 49ers went on to win their first NFL Championship on that day, 26–21. It turned out to be one of the most watched TV broadcasts ever, with more than eighty-five million viewers tuning in. The Nielsen rating was a Super Bowl record of 49.1 with a whopping 73 share. That Super Bowl game was also a milestone for us because it marked the introduction of the "CBS Chalkboard," which would later become known as the "Telestrator." John could use it to diagram and explain football plays for viewers. John has his own distinct style of drawing with lines and arrows and circles going all over the place. I once noted on the air that his scribbles looked to me like "a Chinese menu." I couldn't read either one of them. At first, we had to use a stylus to operate the Telestrator, which was attached to the monitor. But that set-up was too restrictive because you couldn't draw on the far corners of the screen. Then the network improved it to allow John to use his fingertips to draw, and that's when he really got into it with his fingers flying.

While some felt that John had the tendency to get off on tangents on the air, it was just his enthusiasm for the game. If he went on too long, I just "tagged" him, coming in behind one of John's comments to summarize ("tag") it with a very brief sentence. For example, John would be raving about a great juggling, acrobatic catch a receiver had made. I'd tag it with something like, "That guy should've been a waiter."

Then he would move on to another topic. He is great at finding interesting elements to talk about, while I always felt more comfortable listening and then responding to him and to the game. Some people called my style "understated." I've always taken that as a compliment.

Of course, others noted that my off-the-field life was, for many years, out of control. And some had fun with that reputation, too. In the mid-1980s, I walked into The Meadowland's stadium in New Jersey to talk with Coach Bill Parcells for a pregame interview. I found him smoking a cigarette under the stands. He watched me approach as if he had been expecting me. I knew Parcells from his days as an assistant football coach at Army, where he was also assistant basketball coach under Bobby Knight.

"Pat, can I see you about something?" he asked with a concerned expression.

We walked over to his office. He picked up a letter addressed to me and written on pink stationery. "I don't know why this was delivered here," he said to me. "I guess they didn't know how to find you. I didn't read it, but my secretary opened it. I think you ought to read it."

I opened the letter. "Dear Pat," it started. "I don't know if you remember the days when you were with the Giants and you were training up at Bear Mountain. I was working at The Lodge there and we went out a few times . . ."

Yes, I thought, *I definitely remember you.*

It continued, "We lost contact over the years, but I think you should know something. I never told you at the time we were going out that I had herpes—I probably should have told you that."

But that wasn't all. Reading on, I got to the real bomb: "I also never told you that we have a son."

I felt the blood drain from my face as that news sank in. I looked up at Parcells, who was still standing there. I noticed a slight smirk on his face. Only then did I realize what was going on.

It turned out that there was a public relations guy with the Giants, Ed Croke, who had been with the team when I was a player. He had filled in Parcells on the brief fling I'd had with the woman who worked at The Lodge at Bear Mountain. Then the coach concocted the story and had his secretary write me the bogus letter.

It was a humorous but humbling moment. There would be more.

FOX'S DEN

In December 1993, CBS lost the NFL rights to Rupert Murdoch's fledging Fox Network. Fox offered $1.58 billion for the NFC rights—then a record, and a heck of a lot more than the $290 million offered by CBS. There was just one problem for Fox: it didn't have a sports department.

John joked that they shouldn't call it Fox Sports: "They should call it Fox Sport because they have only one sport—NFL football."

But the network set out to remedy that in a hurry. One of their first moves was to hire John and me away from CBS. Terry Bradshaw, Dick Stockton, and James Brown followed. In fact, most of the key people from our old CBS broadcasting and production crews were lured to Fox. We were very glad—make that relieved—to be joined by our veteran director-producer team of Sandy Grossman and Bob Stenner. John and I got all the airtime and most of the credit, but Sandy and Bob were the two guys who pulled everything together and made us look good. They were not only our broadcast teammates and traveling companions, they were true friends.

Bob, a big handsome single guy, was the perfect television producer and lead man, as well as a great dinner companion and legendary ladies' man. Unfortunately, the stories that go into the making of the legend must go untold here. He'll have to write his own book. Sandy was more of a family man, but also a diligent, hard-working guy who was considered the best in the business. Neither of them could be intimidated or overwhelmed by the incredible demands and pressures of their jobs. Both of them became experts on football and the intricacies of the sport. They knew our strengths and our weaknesses, and they played to them perfectly. It was a joy to work with them both at CBS and with our new employer.

It was an emotional time for me, and for a lot of other long-time CBS people who were leaving. I had been associated with CBS since 1960, and it had been a wonderful ride with some priceless memories. Yet Fox picked up its football coverage where CBS left off. John and I remained the NFL's signature tandem, and no one suggested that we tweak anything. John did get a fancier, high-tech Madden Cruiser out of the move.

In our days in the Fox fold, John and I cruised and had a great deal of fun. We did our share of one-sided games; when the games got dull, we really stepped up. We could have fun and make it interesting talking about a leaking water bucket, a bird on the field, a hot dog, a fat couple in the stands, and, of course, our annual Thanksgiving trademark: the famous six-legged Turducken, one of the ugliest holiday birds ever to be stuffed and consumed.

The tradition began when a New Orleans fan visited the Madden Cruiser and offered to make us a Thanksgiving meal like we'd never had before. He succeeded. Though it looked like a couple of good birds gone bad, it tasted mighty fine. I lucked out if a piece was left for me.

John and I called eight Super Bowl games in our twenty-one years together as the NFL's big-game tandem. Number eight, the seventeenth Super Bowl broadcast of my career, came on February 3, 2002, in a squeaker between the New England Patriots and the St. Louis Rams. It was our last game together. Fox informed us before the game that they wanted to split us up.

There were several theories advanced about the network's motives. John and I pondered the how and the why of it together, but there wasn't much we could do about it. Neither of us wanted it to happen, and both of us were deeply saddened when it did. At the time, I think John knew he was going to get an offer to do *Monday Night Football* on ABC because the network's experiment with comedian Dennis Miller as "color man" was over.

Monday Night Football promised to give John an even bigger national stage, which he richly deserved. He never said that was the case—I just sensed it. As it turns out, John did get the ABC offer, and he accepted it less than a month later.

It was tough to handle the breakup of our team. After John left Fox they offered me a job to work games. However, they weren't the A-games, and people I trusted said that I probably would not be happy after being on the main stage for so long. While John wanted to do prime time, I liked Sunday afternoon games because those broadcasts were more focused on football. Monday night is more show business and entertainment. I was just not as comfortable with that concept.

In our time in the booth together, John and I broadcast around 450 NFL games. As I was preparing for and calling Super Bowl XXXVI, I knew I'd miss standing next to Big John, watching his antics and enjoying (and reacting to) his commentary. At the end of the fourth quarter during that final broadcast, John saluted me on the air, calling me "a national treasure."

I told him that they could take me out of the booth but they'd never take away the times we'd had together.

It was a bittersweet ending, but I realized there would be more football seasons ahead for me. It was fitting that our final Super Bowl together had a storybook ending as the game came down to a last-second field goal. My call of that kick was as simple and sparse as ever: "It's right down the pipe. Adam Vinatieri . . . no time on the clock, and the New England Patriots have won Super Bowl thirty-six. Unbelievable!"

My time with John Madden had been just that. Unbelievable . . . and wonderful, too.

CHAPTER EIGHT

MASTERS MEMORIES

LONG BEFORE I BECAME THE VOICE OF CBS GOLF, I HAD TO PASS A TEST for which there were no hard-and-fast answers—and no evident preparation. I definitely could have used the *Cliffs Notes* for this one.

The test was offered like a dose of medicine by an eccentric Wall Street executive, not far from the eighteenth green at Augusta National Golf Club. Cliff Roberts, who cofounded the storied club with golfing legend Bobby Jones, Jr., was the man to see if you wanted to call the Masters. And there I was, in the early spring of 1968, on my way to an "audience" with the tournament's intimidating founding director.

At that point in my career, I was as confident as any sports broadcaster in the network ranks. But the thought of meeting Roberts made me more than a little skittish. If Roberts didn't like me, I wouldn't get the assignment. CBS had nothing to say about it. My network was televising the Masters on a year-to-year handshake agreement with the club. The CBS brass was terrified of losing their rights to the enormously popular and prestigious event. Even more, they were terrified of Roberts, who relished his tight-fisted dictatorship in this small but gorgeously landscaped corner of the universe.

Though he was a brilliant businessman, Roberts saw Augusta National as his life's crowning achievement. Thirty-seven years before our first meeting, he and Jones partnered to buy the property, a 365-acre flower nursery that had served as an indigo plantation before the Civil War. Roberts, a stockbroker who managed Jones's investments, came up with the idea of making the property an exclusive national golf club with limited local membership. The problem with this strategy was that the Great Depression still gripped the nation. Roberts and the other founders soon realized they'd need a big PR blitz to sell the place to the country's movers and shakers.

Roberts and Jones chose the Augusta location because it was midway for most of the major league baseball teams in cities of the Northeast and Midwest on their way to spring-training camps in Florida. The new club worked to lure sportswriters into Augusta on their drives, train rides, or bus trips back to New York, Boston, Chicago, Cleveland, and other cities. Wisely, the club timed their golf tournament for early April to catch the writers en route.

Word spread quickly in the sporting press about this magnificent new layout and tournament in Georgia, which in turn caught the fancy of preeminent businesses throughout the country. An Augusta National membership became the ultimate corporate status symbol and a certified mark of pure manhood.

Like many of my contemporaries, I'd wanted to do golf broadcasts because the process looked so simple and relaxing (it isn't), and because I enjoyed playing the game. Other announcers told me that working from Augusta National was like broadcasting from Westminster Abbey; there was such reverence toward the course, and the members took so much pride in making it a first-class experience.

The moment I set foot on the grounds—a golf country club set down in a botanical garden—I saw what they'd been raving about. I'd been on many golf courses, but never had I seen more pristinely manicured grounds. Every tree, shrub, and blade of grass radiated beauty and Southern gothic mystique.

ENTRANCE EXAM

As I made my way past the classic clubhouse and the legendary giant oak tree to Roberts' cabin, I had no idea what to expect. I knocked meekly and entered.

I was surprised to find that he was very slightly built and unimposing physically. He didn't look like a tough guy—but then, neither did Julius Caesar. Roberts made up for his lack of muscle with a steely demeanor that matched the steel-gray of his hair. Standing before him wasn't so much like being called into the principal's office, it was more like being commanded to appear before the pope.

After a brief exchange of pleasantries, Roberts asked, "Would you like something to drink, son?"

"Yes, sir; that would be nice."

I had heard Roberts was a Scotch drinker. I greatly disliked Scotch. Whiskey, preferably Jack Daniels, was my beverage of choice in the winter, vodka in the summer. But this was his domain, and I wanted desperately to be admitted. So when Roberts asked me what I drank, my reply was: "Whatever you are having, Mr. Roberts."

He poured me a tall Scotch in a big silver glass, and I acted pleased to accept it.

There followed a lingering silence. Leaves rustled. The sun crept across the sky. My inquisitor sat stone-faced, apparently deep in thought.

"Son," he finally said. "You know, more people know you from football than they do from golf."

"I'm aware of that, Mr. Roberts," I replied. "But I know golf. I play golf. I've been around the game a lot, sir."

More silence broken only by the sound of ice clinking in my glass as I nervously choked down some of Mr. Roberts's premium Scotch. A couple of good belts did little to ease my jitters.

I nearly jumped out of my seat when he spoke again.

"What is your handicap?"

"Around ten or twelve, sir."

He seemed to enter my numbers into some mental mathematical formula. I tried without success to read his eyes for the results of his calculations.

Finally, he delivered the results.

"Well, son, the best announcer we've ever had here was Chris Schenkel, and he was an eighteen. So you'll be okay."

He dismissed me with a nod of his Scotch glass. I rose, shook his hand, set down my glass, and walked out. I had passed the Cliff Roberts test, presumably. It was simple, yet surreal. I kept thinking, *What if I had been a twenty handicapper?*

ROOKIE TOUR

There were other peculiar rites of passage required in the elite field of golf broadcasting. Before I could step onto the course at Augusta, I had to prove that I could handle the unique challenges of broadcasting golf tournaments.

At my first opportunity I phoned the network's golf producer, Frank Chirkinian, to ask a few perfunctory questions about my duties, such as where and with whom I was to check in. After those were answered, I said, "Oh, and I'm sorry to ask you this, but how do you spell your last name?"

"That's Chirkinian—it's Armenian. You spell it T-A-L-E-N-T. And don't you ever forget it!"

Egos were the biggest hazard in the golf kingdom, it seemed. When I had my first face-to-face meeting with the mercurial CBS golf guru, I realized why he was the boss. He had an instinctive feel for presenting this deceptively difficult sport to a television audience.

"Remember, television is a visual medium," he said. "You don't have to tell people what they can see. Tell 'em something they can't see. People can see that a golfer made the putt. If I ever hear you say, 'He made the putt,' I'll fire you on the spot."

Gotcha. Dramatic presentation seemed to be another hallmark of golf broadcasting. However, there was wisdom in his counsel, and I heeded his advice throughout my career; not just in golf broadcast but in all sports. "Avoid the obvious" was the Chirkinian mantra. Give your viewers color, texture, and background instead.

Blunt and bright, Chirkinian dispensed orders to his team loud and dirty. He rode our backs like a jockey and whipped at us until we found the pace he set. He loved it when someone gave as good as he got. So I dubbed him "the Ayatollah," after the fiery Iranian dictator. It stuck, and I'm certain that Chirkinian was flattered by its dark connotations.

God love him, Chirkinian did everything with dictatorial flair, even the countdown to air time for our CBS golf broadcasts: "Standby, fifteen seconds . . . Comin' to you in ten . . . five seconds . . . Okay, now sing to me, you gray-haired %#@*!"

And sing we did.

Frank was an equal-opportunity abuser. His tirades were just his way of letting us know he cared for us. He treated each of us with equal disdain. Yet it was all a game. He was the driving dad, the hard-nosed coach, the intimidating drill sergeant, and the demanding professor of the CBS golf team. He was the guy who made you better, and you learned to love him as soon as you stopped cursing his birth.

One night in Flint, Michigan, during the Buick Open, he and I were walking back to one of the few decent hotels in town after dinner and drinks. Chirkinian, who'd had a few, looked at me and said, "Pat, I just want ya to know, you big *#&^, that I love ya!" Then he slapped me on the back and hugged me.

"Well, Frank, I love you, too."

There we were, in the middle of downtown Flint, standing on the middle of the sidewalk, hugging one another like long-lost friends. Out of nowhere, a cop appeared.

"Excuse me, boys. I don't know where you two are from, but here in Flint two men don't hug each other in public like that."

We laughed until our ribs ached.

HAZARDS AND TRAPS

Broadcasting a major golf tournament is not nearly as easy as it might appear. In fact, it is by far the toughest assignment for most sportscasters. What do you say when a guy makes a putt? "That's a birdie," or "That's a par," or "It puts him two out of the lead."

The announcer's options are limited. The same goes when a player is out on the fairway. "He's 165 yards out. He's got an eight-iron. He should come in from left to right." That's stock stuff. To enhance it, you have to be creative—take a step out. You talk about the wind, the lie, recent changes in his swing, or what he's likely discussing with his caddy. It's not neurosurgery, but it's more difficult than many broadcast assignments.

Football was much easier. While there are twenty-two players on the field, there's only a finite number of things you need to keep up with: the score, the time on the clock, the down, and so on. Then you call the plays as they happen. You don't have to struggle for things to talk about because there is so much going on. Basketball's even quicker. You just follow the ball while keeping track of the ten players on the court.

The downtime is a killer in golf. You've got to fill it with either brilliance or bull. When things slow down, you may have to go into a golfer's history, talk about his family and his struggles and triumphs. It's bad enough when the leader of a tournament is an established pro whose every step up the ladder has been endlessly described. The biggest challenges come when you find yourself scrambling for any tidbits or scraps of information about a no-name upstart who rises out of the pond muck and surges to the top of the leader board. You might have memorized volumes of detailed biography for every other player in a tournament, then one guy fresh off the Hooter's Tour catches fire with four straight birdies and you can't even pronounce his name.

Golf can make grown men look like fools whether you are swinging a club or manning a microphone. But even on your worst days, it beats toting watermelons across a dusty field in the summer sun. Think about it. The worst thing that can happen on a given day of golf coverage is a sudden change of wardrobe by the participants.

In the morning before the round starts, I would go out to watch players on the practice tees and greens and I'd make a color chart noting that Tom Watson was wearing a red shirt and khaki pants and Arnold Palmer was in a white shirt with yellow pants. That way, during the round, you can make out who is in each group as they comes up the fairway, before the cameras pick them up. But if it started to rain, the golfers stopped and donned their rain gear, making my color chart as worthless as a sand wedge on a par five tee. So I tried to cover my assignment by learning to identify the tour players by their walks, their waggles, their swings, and their caddies.

PAIRINGS

Once again, I was fortunate to rub elbows with some of the best golf broadcasters in the business early in my career. Henry Longhurst and golfing great Byron Nelson were calling CBS golf events when I first gained admission to the sport. "Lord Byron" was not one of those broadcasters who had a hard time thinking of things to say. He has an encyclopedic knowledge of the game, and he is not stingy with golf tips, either.

Not long after George H. W. Bush—an avid golfer—left office, I flew on a private plane with the former president, Byron Nelson, and his wife, Peggy, from Little Rock to College Station. As we were taking off, the senior Bush said to Byron, "Would you mind if I asked you a question about golf?"

"Of course not, Mr. President," Byron answered.

"How can I get more distance out of my eight-iron?" Bush asked.

The former commander in chief got what may have been the most detailed briefing of his personal and political life. Byron is known as one who can tell you every shot hit in every tournament, which way the wind was blowing, and what kind of lie he had. He was not about to short-change Bush. Our flight touched down in College Station with Byron still answering the president's question.

Another great golfer who retired from broadcasting in 2002, Ken Venturi, was the consummate pro in the booth and on the course, and he was also one of the great teachers of both the game's fundamentals and its finer points. He won the 1964 U.S. Open, and there is no telling what he would have done if he hadn't been forced to retire prematurely due to an injury. Ken's experience in the Masters and its impact on his life confirmed for me the importance of that tournament to golf professionals.

Unfortunately, Ken's loss to Arnold Palmer in the 1958 Masters haunted him. They were playing together in the final round when Palmer got a favorable ruling on an embedded ball behind the twelfth hole on the course's famous "Amen Corner." The ruling was delivered two full holes after Palmer apparently double-bogeyed the hole. An official denied Palmer relief from the lie, but Palmer thought he was wrong, so he played a second ball and made par with that while appealing the official's ruling. His appeal was upheld, and Palmer was allowed to record the par.

Venturi complained that Palmer's "3" was illegal because Palmer didn't invoke his right to play the second ball until holing out the first, but in the end Venturi signed off on the score instead of challenging the ruling.

Still, it stuck in his craw for decades. I worked with Ken for many years, and the Masters incident with Palmer came up virtually every time we went out, especially after he got a few glasses of wine in him. If it wasn't the topic of conversation, he would bring it up at some point.

Although he never came out and accused Palmer of cheating, Venturi—who lost the 1956 Masters by one stroke as an amateur after leading through three rounds—remained bitter and resurrected the controversy in a 2004 book. He said course cofounders Bobby Jones and Cliff Roberts told him later that Palmer wasn't entitled to the drop, and Venturi speculated that the ruling went in Palmer's favor because Palmer was such a fan favorite. Venturi's lingering bitterness underscores how important this tournament is to the men who make the cut.

COMIC RELIEF

Thankfully, there are also those who don't take their golf so seriously. Some even regard it as a good walk spoiled. Long before comedian Bill Murray became golf's unofficial course jester, another professional quipster sat with me in the broadcast booth at Pebble Beach.

The late comedian Phil Harris was a close friend of singer Bing Crosby, who founded "The Crosby," the national golf event that pairs professionals with amateurs on one of the world's most gorgeous—and most challenging—golf courses. More recently known as the AT&T Pebble Beach National Pro-Am, this tournament is always entertaining because of the mixed bag of serious golfers, amateurs, and celebrities trying to play together on the bewitching but devilish course.

When Phil Harris joined us in the tower, he usually brought an entourage that included a designated driver, a designated laugher—yes, that's all he did—and a designated pourer. Like me, Phil was a Jack Daniels man. He could go through a quart of Jack Daniels in an afternoon. So it's not surprising that he provided some memorable and some just plain embarrassing moments on the air.

Phil was a good golfer who actually won the Crosby one year with his pro partner; yet he was unpredictable due to his drinking. Once, just as a group was approaching the eighteenth hole beneath our tower, Phil stood up. He'd been sitting between me and Venturi. Our microphones were on, but it didn't bother Phil. He rose, uprooting all the wires attached to his headset in the process and turning over everything, including our water, his whiskey, and all the notes we had in front of us.

Unfazed, Phil leaned over to me and my live microphone and said, "I love you, baby, but I gotta go take a leak."

Phil also came to the Crosby loaded with jokes. He prepared them, and then he'd have me and Venturi set him up with leading questions. One afternoon, when we had a little dead time, I played along: "Phil, what did you do last night?"

"I couldn't find anybody so I went back to my room," he replied.

"What did you do, watch TV?"

"No, I don't like television. I was looking for something to read. The only thing I could find was a Gideon's Bible," the comedian said.

"Really? Did you read it?"

"I opened it up, and there on the fly leaf it's written out, 'If you think you have a drinking problem, call this number.'"

"Did you call?"

"Yeah, it was a liquor store."

HUMBLING GAME

Not all of the humor in golf was scripted, of course. Even in a sport where the players often take their games and themselves very seriously, the gods of laughter cannot be denied. I was in Orlando working the Citrus Open, and my old University of Arkansas buddy Miller Barber had an early tee time. I didn't go on the air until much later so I went out to follow his group and give him a little encouragement.

Barber's caddy was Herman Miller, a large man who later gained notoriety as Lee Trevino's caddy. Herman was struggling in the heat, especially since the tournament had issued heavy orange overalls to all caddies for the event. But Herman found a way to air-condition his overalls. On the second hole, Miller ran in a sixty-foot putt for a birdie. After celebrating, he asked Herman to get the ball. When Herman bent down to get it, his overalls were no longer over all. He split them all the way down the back. That was a real problem because Herman wasn't wearing any underwear. The caddy's backside was exposed on the course's front side.

Trying to keep his mind on the game, Miller asked a tournament official to radio for a backup set of overalls. In the meantime, Herman tried to position Miller's bag strategically over the malfunction in his wardrobe. His boss bogeyed the next hole, and it appeared his play was being affected by the distraction. After the fifth hole, Miller asked the tournament official if he could borrow his radio. He put out a Mayday.

"Will you guys at headquarters get me some help out here? My caddy tore his pants three holes ago, and I ain't been able to putt since then because of the flies!"

Veteran golf professional Gary McCord was a colorful, though not very successful, member of the PGA tour. He became a member of the CBS team and was known for his outspokenness, but Gary was very subdued when he went along with us on one of our annual visits to golf legend Ben Hogan. We made the trek each year prior to the Colonial National Invitation Tournament held on Hogan's beloved Shady Oaks Country Club in Fort Worth. McCord was eager to meet the elderly Hogan, so I introduced him as soon as we were seated.

"I didn't catch your name," Hogan said to him.

McCord introduced himself again.

"And what do you do, son?" Hogan asked.

"I play on the PGA tour, sir," McCord said.

"How long have you been playing?" Hogan inquired.

"Fifteen years."

"What have you won?" Hogan asked.

"I never won," McCord admitted.

"Fifteen years and you haven't won?" Hogan exclaimed. "Why don't you quit?"

Of course, I had my humbling moments, too. When Joe Ford, Augusta National's vice chairman, introduced me to his wife, she was not overly impressed.

"Pat Summerall? I've heard of you. You're the guy who puts me to sleep every Sunday afternoon."

After that, I did my best to find ways to keep golf wives awake, especially during the Masters.

An even more humbling review came from another former television man, President Ronald Reagan. I had the opportunity to go to the White House. He greeted me warmly, but with a caveat. "Pat, I really like your work," Reagan said. "But I have to tell you, Vin Scully is my favorite announcer."

"Well, thanks a lot, Mr. President!"

MASTERS MAESTROS

I called my first Masters Tournament in 1968 after passing the Cliff Roberts test. It was memorable for me because during that event I met Augusta's other founding partner, the great Bobby Jones. He was only sixty-six, but he was in a wheelchair, suffering from a rare disease that caused progressive paralysis. Yet he was the perfect mild-mannered Southern gentleman and seemed upbeat about life. I was surprised that he still smoked quite a bit, given his condition. Sadly, he died three years later.

Jones's cofounder, Roberts, continued his authoritarian reign until his death in 1977. Suffering from cancer and depression, he took his own life on Augusta's par three course. There are memorials to both Jones and Roberts at Augusta, and their influence is still strongly felt in the clubhouse restaurant, where "Mr. Cliff's" (as Roberts was known by locals) favorite brands of olives and pears are still served at Monday night dinner.

Unlike other tournaments, the Masters—and its tournament chairmen—had tentacles of influence that extended far beyond Augusta, Georgia. CBS bent over backward to accommodate Roberts and the Augusta National, no matter what happened. Roberts was a Wall Street investment banker, and if he held a fund-raiser or other function in the Big Apple, the head of the CBS sports department, Bill MacPhail, made sure we went. As time passed, Roberts and I got to be good friends, while everyone else at the network was still terrified of him.

The network executives did not want to cross the Masters' hosts and risk losing the prestigious event. So, they bowed to every demand. CBS wasn't allowed to expand its Masters coverage as it had for the U.S. Open and other majors. We also had to limit commercials and get final approval for all commercial content from the Masters Tournament office. That's still the case today. None of the bigwigs at CBS could bear the thought of losing the Masters, much less that it might happen under their regimes.

The four tournament chairmen who have succeeded Roberts have been a little more lenient and forgiving, although it was one of Roberts's successors, Jack Stephens, who almost pulled the plug on CBS's Masters coverage. Stephens, who mostly stayed out of the spotlight during his seven years as tourney chairman, was reportedly angry with CBS for some undisclosed affront. NBC and ABC caught wind of it and were hovering around, politicking to take over coverage. Stephens heard their cases, although CBS managed to placate him and hold on to the coveted broadcast rights.

SOUTHERN MANNERS

The tournament in Augusta is built around both a gorgeous landscape and a tradition of respect and graciousness. Guided by those principles, it has always been the best-run tournament on tour. And once you get inside, it is a very comfortable and reasonable place to spend a few days.

Concession prices are amazingly low. You can get one of Augusta National's famous egg-salad or pimiento-cheese sandwiches for about a buck. And it's faster than McDonalds, too. I overheard one of the tournament organizers saying, "Well, last year in the pimiento-cheese line, it took an average of three minutes to get through. We better cut that down. We need to sell it in more places."

Augusta National is also home to the most polite fans in sports. You can enter the country club at 6:30 in the morning when the gates open, leave your chair and blanket in a good vantage point on the eighteenth hole, go out on the course and watch the rest of the tournament, then return to the eighteenth, and find your chair and blanket undisturbed.

Respect is demanded of broadcasters at the Masters. Each year, the announcers would meet with club members on the Masters Television Committee, and though the committee didn't exactly tell us what to say, they did tell us what not to say. To this day, announcers can't mention what brands of shoes or clothes a player is wearing or what equipment he is using. That would be free advertising. You can't broach the subject of money, either. For example, you can't say, "That putt means X amount of dollars to him," or "A par will put him twenty-fifth on the money list." That's because you don't know exactly how much prize money will be given out anyway until all the concessions and souvenir proceeds are tallied—and those are considerable. But you don't dare venture a guess on the air.

Unlike other invitational golf tournaments, the Masters has its own unique method of selecting who gets to tee it up, and we were not allowed to speculate on how that process worked. The Augusta National members ran a very tight ship. I was often reminded that we were to use only "appropriate" and positive language on the air during our broadcasts of the event. We could talk all we wanted to about the weather and the trees and the camellias and the azaleas. One CBS announcer forgot himself—at least in the eyes of Roberts—and he paid the price. In 1966, Jack Whitaker referred to the crowd at a Monday playoff between Gene Littler and Billy Casper as a "mob" that had left behind an inordinate amount of "garbage." Roberts and the Augusta brass took exception to this and banned Jack from future coverage. The Masters didn't have a "mob," they had "patrons," CBS was told. Nor did they have garbage; they had "debris."

That littering incident truly was an aberration; many club members and security people had departed Augusta Sunday night or early Monday to go back to their real jobs. Most of the season badge holders also had to leave, and they sold or gave their badges away to people who ordinarily couldn't get in, including some rowdies—resulting in those "mob" and "garbage" characterizations. Chirkinian told me that Augusta National was so embarrassed that things had spun out of control that the tournament took it out on Whitaker. When Longhurst got sick several years later, Chirkinian brought Whitaker into Roberts's office and asked if he could use him to replace the Englishman. Roberts quickly agreed as a way to make amends.

Even after the reign of the stern Roberts, Augusta National's leadership kept firm control on our broadcasts. During my last Masters telecast in 1994, CBS analyst Gary McCord said the incredibly fast greens looked as though they'd been "bikini-waxed." He then joked about "body bags" that were hidden behind the seventeenth green for those golfers unlucky enough to hit over it. McCord was removed from Masters coverage by the Augusta brass, and he never returned.

I was always very careful in my broadcasts at the Masters, but I had at least one minor critic. Chirkinian once showed me a letter that upbraided me for getting the course geography wrong:

> The announcer at thirteen said a ball landed in Ray's Creek. That is not Ray's Creek. The stream that runs across thirteen is a tributary of Ray's Creek.

I stood corrected! Any broadcaster who ever worked there, it seemed, endured some sort of correction or hand slap or censure. But we all kept coming back because we loved the tournament, we loved Augusta National, and we loved the unique atmosphere.

RETURN OF THE BEAR

My most emotional and memorable experience as a broadcaster came during the dramatic final round in 1986 when Jack Nicklaus won it at age forty-six. Most golf sportswriters and other wags had written him off as too old to accomplish the feat, so the retired athlete in me was pulling for him.

After you've been to the Masters a few years, you learn to read the sounds of the crowds to determine their moods and their favorite players. The roars during that final round for Nicklaus were just incredibly uplifting. Known as "the Golden Bear" in his prime, when he'd won five Masters, he'd entered this one after struggling with his game so that few gave him a chance of getting another green jacket.

With just ten holes left to play, Nicklaus was six shots behind leader Seve

Ballesteros. But he birdied nine, then ten, then eleven. From the broadcast tower on the elevated eighteenth green, we heard the rumblings from the valley growing louder and louder with each hole. When Jack eagled fifteen, we realized something extraordinary was happening.

Still on fire, Jack birdied sixteen and seventeen, and walked to the eighteenth tee needing only a par to post a phenomenal thirty on the back nine—giving him his sixth green jacket.

When he started up the eighteenth fairway with his son, Jackie, caddying for him, it was as if a huge sound wave was rising up and pouring over that final hill. With every step, it seemed, the roar rose another decibel. It was a scene that was so emotionally charged that I couldn't speak through the entire hole, not even when he sank his winning putt.

It was that rare occasion when even I was swept up in the emotion of a grand event, an incredible shining moment. We were witnessing one of sport's most glorious victories. I had been a professional broadcaster for more than a quarter century at the time, but I was choked up and speechless for the first time.

For years after that, Jack and I spent hours reliving that extraordinary moment. I don't know who has more fond recollections of it, him or me.

Yes, Augusta National supplied me with many memories that will last a lifetime. But not all of them, I'm humbled to say, were glorious.

CHAPTER NINE

THE RECKONING

I AWOKE IN A GUESTHOUSE IN AUGUSTA, GEORGIA, A SERENE AND beautiful place that is home to my favorite sporting event in the world. But I felt disoriented, queasy, and panicked. It was 3 a.m., and something was terribly wrong with me. I struggled to roll out of bed and staggered into the bathroom. I'd gotten sick from too much drinking before—far too many times to count—but this was different. As I knelt on the bathroom floor, I felt as if my insides were pouring out on waves of the vodka I'd consumed before collapsing into my bed.

My drinking had increased in recent months, and now the penalties were getting steeper. There was blood in my vomit. A few years earlier I'd had a similar episode. I'd bled so badly that I had to be hospitalized. I was sick for most of the night, coughing up mostly blood. This continued on and off the rest of the night. Doctors found a severe ulcer—caused, they said, by many years of heavy drinking. I missed several game broadcasts because of that episode.

My bosses at CBS quietly expressed their concern. It should have been a wake-up call for me. It was taking less and less for me to get drunk, another bad sign. After that, I drank very little in public. I simply hid my drinking, pouring myself drinks in the privacy of my hotel room or wherever I was staying—like this house in Augusta.

I drew deep breaths and tried to compose myself, but I still couldn't fight the waves of nausea. I lowered my dizzy head once more. What the hell was I doing to myself? Finally, I got back on my feet and staggered over to the sink to splash water on my face. As I looked in the mirror, the fluorescent lights around the medicine cabinet seemed to grow brighter and brighter. They illuminated my pale and haggard face, my bloodshot eyes, and all the protruding veins on my face and my nose. I looked like a monster. I was repulsed at my own image, at once terrified and disgusted.

My entire body was in revolt. I threw up again and again. There was more blood and what appeared to be tissue. Good Lord, could that be stomach lining? I shuffled over to the mirror again, propping myself up on the sink, almost afraid to see if the ghostly face I had seen earlier could really have been me. I looked at my reflection, and the hard truth came back to light. The mirror hadn't lied. I looked hideous, and the lights seemed to intensify that effect. It was as if I was staring into the face of death. *Is this the way you want to look the rest of your life? Is this the way you want to live?*

After an hour of staring into the mirror and heaving into the toilet, I made a solemn vow: "I'm never going to take another drink."

WARNINGS

Dawn came and I had to face the world. This would not be an easy proposition. I had arrived in town the night before for the 1992 Masters Tournament. I was staying at a rented house, as was the custom for tour players and TV people during tournament week. My first course of business had been to stock up on party supplies at the liquor store for the annual weeklong festivities—a priority in just about every city I traveled to these days.

I often had joked that the secret to a long and happy life was to drink

Jack Daniels when it was cold and Smirnoff Vodka when it was hot. Recreational drinking, after all, was a big part of the sports-broadcasting scene. At football and basketball games, there were free drinks everywhere. At golf and tennis tournaments, everybody had a hospitality suite, so you could load up anytime you wanted to. And I had done that with frequency. When the broadcast day was done, I was often the first one at the bar and the last one to leave it. But somewhere along the miles I'd traveled, the focus of the parties had changed from fun and relaxation to total intoxication. I still called it partying, but it was drinking to get drunk, and I couldn't run fast enough to avoid the effects it was having on my body and my mental health.

En route to Augusta National later that morning, my driver had to pull over so that I did not throw up in his vehicle. How I got through that day, I don't know. I don't remember much about it. I had a few things to do to prepare for the broadcasts that weekend, and I did them on autopilot. The entire day passed in a blur of nausea and guilt. I was living drink to drink and my body was breaking down.

The constant boys' night out lifestyle had caught up to me, just as I'd been warned it would. Coworkers, friends, and acquaintances had tried to sound the alarm. A couple of CBS people had pulled me aside and encouraged me to cut back on the booze, hinting that they thought it was affecting my work. The wife of a good friend had stepped up, too: "Why don't you slow down a little bit, Pat? You don't have to drink the most. You're a public figure. People are watching you. Slow down."

But the truth was that I couldn't stop drinking. Alcoholism plays tricks on you. It's a disease that is insidious and self-perpetuating. It makes promises that you can't keep. And so I broke my "solemn oath" and hit the bottle again. I resumed my drinking through the rest of the week, falling into the flow. However, for the first time I had the constant awareness that I could not afford to keep it up much longer.

Augusta during the Masters might be the worst place in the world to try and quit drinking. There were always parties and free booze and plenty of excitement. Freddie Couples won his first major that week, while Mark Calcavecchia blistered the back nine with a twenty-nine in the last round. It was a very good tournament, but I was a little numb to it all because of the inner turmoil.

On the Monday after the tournament, I left Augusta for Philadelphia to narrate a Minnesota Vikings highlights video for NFL Films and to tape a series of TV commercials that required more than one hundred voice-overs. In the car, I got the call from Brookie that marked the beginning of the end of my drinking days, and a new course for my life.

The intervention was a wrenching, heartbreaking, and profoundly embarrassing event in my life. I will be forever grateful for it, even though I still deal with all of the painful feelings it recalls. I'm still surprised—as was everyone else at the time—that I agreed to go to the Betty Ford Clinic that day. My decision shocked everyone. Most thought I was too proud or too arrogant to admit that my drinking had become a problem. But that guesthouse mirror in Augusta had shown me what others were seeing, and the bloody vomit was an alarming sight that I could not get out of my mind. Introspection and contemplation had never been my strong suits, but there were forces bearing down that were too powerful to ignore.

THE TREATMENT

Had I been counting my blessings, my friends certainly should have been near the top of the list. One of them, Brookie, couldn't stand the thought of me flying alone on the plane to Palm Springs. Maybe he was afraid that I might jump out in midair.

When we arrived at the airport, Brookie had a surprise for me. He announced that he'd had the plane that was taking me to the Betty Ford

Clinic stocked with Jack Daniels (my favorite) and vodka (his). "Just in case you want to have one last blowout," he said.

But I wasn't in the mood, nor was he. It was a very long flight to Palm Springs, California, but neither of us touched a drop, nor did we say much to each other. I had been through an emotional gauntlet, and thoughts of what would come next were racing through my mind. *Is this going to be like jail? What about my work? What will people say? Will I be able to handle it? If I stop drinking, will I have anyone to laugh with anymore? Has my drinking really gotten bad enough to merit something this extreme?*

Then, just as I got myself worked up, I'd remember the blood, the retching, my ghastly face in the mirror, and—worst of all—my Susie's letter. My daughter was ashamed of me. Enough is enough.

Still, I wasn't ready to fully acknowledge that I was an alcoholic, which is typical of someone who has just gone through an intervention. After a brief period of guilt and remorse, my demons regained their hold and convinced me that I was a victim of some sort of conspiracy. When I finally arrived at Betty Ford, the anger had set in once again. I groused to anyone in earshot that those who had turned me in were doing it for their own selfish reasons. I spared no one my bile. I'd been betrayed.

As the professional staff at the clinic welcomed me, I treated them like jailers. When my counselor, Tom Martin, introduced himself, I just grunted. A little later, I asked him if the Jeep with the New York Giants wheel cover that I had noticed parked outside was his. It was, he said. *Good*, I thought. *He's a big Giants fan. This is going to be easy.*

But Tom was unrelenting. He told me repeatedly that I had to be honest and direct, or this wasn't going to work. Still, I continued to push the boundaries with him. One day, one of the Betty Ford Center's big benefactors—a member of the board of directors—came in to visit me. He started smoking, which I knew Tom had silently observed. So I confronted my counselor later.

"I wanna say something, Tom. You're always talking about being honest. You were in the room with that donor. He started smoking, which is against the rules in here, and you never said a word to him. Not one word."

Tom replied, "That's true, Pat. All I can say is, I chose not to die on that mountain today."

Initially they told me my "treatment" would last twenty-eight days, but my stay turned out to be longer. I was so angry and unresponsive the first five days that the counselors refused to count that period toward my treatment. My deep well of hostility was the biggest hurdle. Long before I got there, my counselor figured out that most high profile, accomplished men are trained to quash their emotions and get the job done. If they don't, they're out. This was especially true of me, a professional athlete, who could ill afford to show any signs of weakness. Tom also knew that, coming from a broken family, I had likely shut a lot of emotional doors as a way to cope with reality. Now, he wanted to draw me out, to get me back to my roots so I could sort out my life. Progress was slow.

Then the letters came. One day I walked into Tom's office after my AA and Bible readings, carrying some letters I had received. Tom told me I attracted more letters than anyone who had ever stayed at the center— boxes and boxes of them. But this particular letter was from a cardiac surgeon in North Carolina. "You have been an idol to me," the doctor wrote. "I have followed you throughout your career and I consider you a tremendous man . . ."

A tremendous man?

Such letters were powerful emotional triggers. I told Tom I couldn't believe someone like this surgeon had taken the time to write such a thoughtful and supportive note to me.

I was really blown away by a telephone call that was allowed to come in from the outside. Normally they didn't allow phone calls. But there aren't many people willing to stand up to former Chicago Bears player and coach, Mike Ditka—a tough, tough guy if there ever was one.

I have to give Tom credit. He intercepted the call to be certain that Ditka understood the situation. "Coach, I have to know if you support Pat in this," Tom said bravely.

Ditka said he did. I then talked with him. He told me that I had always been "a man's man" and that he knew I could handle this situation. "You are in the right place," Ditka said. "I'm a hundred percent behind what you are doing."

It was a thoughtful gesture from a great guy. Because of support like that, I gradually grew a little more receptive to the counselors. I lost the attitude and participated in the meetings willingly. Luckily, I never got the DT's or suffered any other severe withdrawal symptoms those first few days. What's more, I was starting to lose my craving for alcohol—and that's not always the case with a lot of alcoholic patients at first. Sometimes the thirst never goes away.

SEEING THE LIGHT

After my initial five-day rant, I grew gradually more receptive to the counselors. Instead of trying to manipulate the situation, I began participating in the meetings with the feeling that I might as well learn something while I was there. The Betty Ford Center is a top-of-the-line addiction facility, but they keep some of the accommodations intentionally sparce. They only give you two books to read—the Alcoholics Anonymous book and the Bible.

I read the AA book a few times and put it aside. But I kept coming back to the Bible. To my surprise I found it engrossing, like some codebook to a world I'd heard about but never delved into. Since the days of Sunday school at the First Methodist Church in Lake City, I'd had no exposure to the Bible. There were guys on some of my pro teams who talked about being Christian, and the Catholic players would often go to Sunday Mass together. But I had little to no interest in religion. Professional football teams are as steeped in the jock mentality as any group you'll likely encounter, and, back then, it was almost a sign of weakness to talk seriously about God or faith. If two guys had equal athletic ability, the non-religious guy was usually considered the superior player.

At the Betty Ford Clinic, it was an entirely different environment. Religion and faith and the teachings in the Bible are integral parts of the recovery program. So there was no avoiding it, and after the first week or so, I was actually intrigued by it. My anger and my desire to drink disappeared. I began to feel more human. I found myself taking an active role in the sessions. Before long, I was leading some of them. A light was coming on.

Never much for introspection, I was being forced to look at life as I never had before. My counselor was relentless, but my emotional walls were tall and thick. Rejected by my parents at a very early age, I'd learned to wall off certain things and just to leave them be. In group counseling sessions, every other male talked about having serious relationship problems with his father and how it was a contributing factor for his alcoholism. And yet, I couldn't blame my father. I certainly had my problems with him, but I simply did not blame him on any conscious level. I had shut him out of my emotional life totally at such a young age, I didn't see how he could be responsible for my current predicament.

FIRST LADY

Early one morning during my stay, I was sitting by the pond at the clinic, enjoying the quiet and watching the ducks swim. In the distance I saw a sprightly woman scurrying about the campus, sprucing up the grounds by picking up little scraps of paper and other litter. She didn't look like a groundskeeper, so I thought she might be a patient trying to make amends. As she got closer, I realized she was neither. It was the former first lady Betty Ford, whose own battle with alcoholism led to the creation of the clinic.

Mrs. Ford had obviously done more than lend her name to the clinic. She was deeply involved and very caring. We struck up a conversation that morning, and I was glad to have someone to talk to. She'd sought me out, she said, because her husband was a fan of mine and wanted to meet me. It was a little surreal to have the wife of a former president of the United States approach me at a rehabilitation center. But then, I'd learned to deal with the surreal. The fact that Mrs. Ford was so open about her own addiction eased any feelings of shame or embarrassment I had.

Gerald Ford came to the center a few days later and I was invited to meet him afterward. As we spoke, he offered encouragement with my treatment and then we moved on to professional football. He was up on the NFL, and he told me a bit about his own football career. President Ford graduated from the University of Michigan, where he was an all-star center and team MVP. He was riding on a train back from the East-West College All-Star game when he met Packers coach Curly Lambeau, the man whose name would ultimately adorn Green Bay's famous stadium. On the spot, Lambeau offered Ford a contract to play for the Packers, but the future president declined.

"I'd like to do that," Ford told him. "But I think I'm going to continue in politics."

He went on to Yale Law School, four years in the navy, and a long and respected political career. You didn't have to know that he'd once served as president of the United States to be impressed with Gerald Ford. He is a rock-solid guy, someone you can count on to do the right thing by instinct. A devoted husband and father, a man of faith and a warm human being, he was someone that I felt I could learn from. We struck up a friendship that continues to this day.

The Fords have even stayed at our house, and you haven't had interesting guests until you have a former president of the United States for a sleepover. He and Betty don't pack lightly. They brought sixteen Secret Service agents to our house for the night. They checked every square inch of the house, and thoroughly screened everyone on our guest lists. We were a little bewildered by it all. When we went to do our customary night check of doors and security alarms, an agent stopped us.

"Mr. Summerall," he said, "would you mind not setting the security?" he asked. "I think we've got it covered."

LIFTING THE CURTAIN

My stay at the Betty Ford Clinic was full of revelations, which I guess is how it was meant to be. It was as if a curtain or veil was being lifted off my perceptions, and I began to see and to understand things clearly for the first time. For example, I had thought drinking made me "better"— both socially and professionally. I had been convinced that I was more gregarious while under the influence—funnier, more outgoing, more popular, more fluid, more charming. Now the truth began to dawn on me: if anything, it was just the opposite.

When I first started in the broadcasting business, I had a reputation of being patient and easy-going. All the younger people wanted to work with me because I wasn't quick to jump on them if they made a mistake. But as the years and the parties passed, I became more erratic in my judgment, and less patient as I drank more frequently and recovered more slowly. In addition, I had lowered my standards along the way—professionally, personally, and physically. To my shame, I had become a practiced liar and a seasoned cover-up man. I was spending more and more time on the road just to be around the party scene, always to the detriment of my family. I had walked away from my marriage and alienated my three kids. They didn't deserve that treatment.

Another thing became clear as the boozy cloud lifted: until I admitted that I had a problem, I wasn't going to make any progress. Going to Betty Ford, getting counseling, attending church—none of it made any difference, not until I was willing to admit I had a problem and to commit to doing something about it. There's a saying at Betty Ford: "Your heart and head should have a meeting in your gut." Only then was I ready to move on to a better life.

Owning up to my weakness in front of other people, even to small groups, was a very difficult and painful thing for me—this tough old NFL guy. The words "My name is Pat Summerall and I'm an alcoholic" weren't easy to say at first. But the more I said them and the more I shared my story, the easier the sessions got, and the better I dealt with my condition. I realized that I desperately needed help, and that all those people who confronted me—as imperfect as they might be themselves—only wanted to help save me from the path of destruction I was on.

I no longer wished ill on any of them, as I had on those first several days there. I realized I couldn't have accomplished my sobriety without their intervention, and I knew they had sacrificed their time and emotional energy to do what they did. We all need help at some point in our lives. As Bill MacPhail, head of CBS sports, said to me years ago, "Somebody in your childhood—and I don't know how you were raised—someone told you what was right and what was wrong. Who told you that?"

The answer, of course, was my grandmother; she had been there for me when my parents weren't. She gave me hope and the will to carry on with my young life, and eventually to thrive in the real world. She was the miracle of my childhood. And the irony did not escape me that her first and middle names, Augusta Georgia, were also the name of the city where I had come face-to-face with some of my greatest moments, as well as with my flawed perspectives and my very mortality. Augusta, it seemed, was guiding me again.

RELATIONSHIP SCARS

As my days at Betty Ford wound down, I felt saved in more ways than one. Night after night, I thought, *I do have a conscience.* Somebody or something is telling me what's right and what's wrong. But who or what is that? We had devotions three or four times a day at Betty Ford, and my curiosity about the existence of a Supreme Being—about God—grew. Though I had prayed on occasion in my playing days—mostly that nobody got hurt—it was perfunctory. I really had no faith. I hadn't gone to church since college, when Kathy—who was a strong Christian—asked me to go with her. But eventually, she went on her own while I was off either playing or broadcasting. We never read the Bible together, and never discussed Christianity or our beliefs.

When my career took off, I left her behind. I claimed that we didn't have much in common anymore. She had married me, the hometown sports' hero, but she had never been much of a sports' fan, and my entire life was built around it. She raised our children virtually on her own. It is one of my greatest regrets that I was not a presence or guide for their lives. I failed them as a father in the most critical years because I was so absorbed in my own career and the celebrity life. My excuse for neglecting Kathy was that I'd changed and grown and she hadn't. If there was any truth to that, it was also true that I had never given her much of a chance to grow with me. Most of the time, I wasn't there—and even when I was around, I lied to her with practiced skill.

In my self-indulgent lifestyle, I didn't see that cheating on my wife was a bad thing. I was enjoying what I was doing too much. Lying didn't bother me; in fact, I was proud that I'd become so skilled at it. I was proud that I was getting away with it. I would have been outraged if she had cheated on me, of course. A lot of men have this strange way of thinking, but it isn't right.

The reality was that I didn't want to hurt Kathy, but I no longer loved her. Kathy and the kids visited me at the Betty Ford Clinic, and we talked on the telephone occasionally while I was there. I appreciated that they supported the treatment and my participation in it. Yet the wounds were very deep. I had hurt her badly with my drinking and my carousing and my absence from the family. Just as I was preparing to leave Betty Ford, she told my counselors that she felt I was not ready to go home. "He's still the same person," she said. I was furious with her for saying that. I wanted to leave. I felt I was ready. I knew I had changed. Yet I could not blame her for striking back at me after all those years of neglect on my part. I went home to her thinking that I wanted to make the marriage work. I owed her an effort. But in truth I loved someone else, and I had for a long time.

SECRET LOVE

I'd met Cheri Burns during the 1978 Colonial National Invitational Tournament in Fort Worth. A mutual acquaintance introduced us. Cheri had grown up in a sports family and she was an NFL fan, which was a big plus. She was initially apprehensive about me, figuring I was arrogant and egotistical and a woman chaser. On the day we were to meet, she was on Colonial's grounds most of the day, but our paths didn't cross as anticipated. She walked into the clubhouse in late afternoon and was climbing the back stairs when she ran into the guy who was trying to set us up. He said, "Where have you been? Pat was here."

Our friend asked her to accompany him into the pro shop, where he proceeded to call me at my hotel just as I got back to my room. He and I talked golf, but I soon broke in and asked if Cheri was still around. Indeed, she was, he said, so I asked him to put her on the phone. I was instantly charmed by her voice and her engaging personality. I invited her and her friends to join us for dinner. Cheri was outgoing and friendly and we hit it off from the start. We left the crowded CBS party and headed for the Waterworks at the Hilton downtown, where we talked and laughed and danced the night away. She was a terrific dancer and before we knew it, the bartender was announcing last call. We shut the place down. I invited Cheri up to the broadcast tower the next day and then out to dinner that night. We are still together.

There is no dancing around one fact: I was still married at the time that I met Cheri. Kathy and I had grown apart emotionally, and we were both hanging on to a bond that had long ago disintegrated, but we were still married. As an accomplished liar, I first told Cheri that I was separated even though when I was not on the road Kathy and I were still living together. I soon told Cheri the truth, and she took it hard. She refused to see me for a time. Cheri had grown up as a straight-laced Southern Baptist girl. But we knew we had something special together. I told her that Kathy and I stayed together for the children's sake, and that my heart was no longer in the marriage. Eventually, Cheri agreed to see me again. Neither one of us could bear the thought of giving up. We had an affair for seventeen years before Kathy and I finally divorced. It was not an ideal situation for any of us. I knew it was wrong at the time, but because of my alcoholism it was easier to live a lie than to do the right thing.

Because of my own parents' failed marriage, I had always said I would never get divorced. It was not something I did easily, or without considerable angst. But my feelings for Cheri were stronger than almost any other force. We married in 1996 with Tom Brookshier at my side as best man. John Madden traveled from California to Dallas in the Madden Cruiser to be at the wedding.

Kathy struggled with our marriage at first, but eventually she accepted it. She told us that she prayed for us. Kathy was a strong believer that Christ's love is about forgiveness and that Christians must practice it. We had a good relationship for the years preceding Kathy's death from cancer in December 2005. I still had some healing to do with my children.

I'm grateful that they've given me the opportunity to finally be a true father to them and a grandfather to their children.

A VOID FILLED

Cheri had never been a heavy drinker, but she joined me in giving up alcohol after I left the Betty Ford Center. She has also become my partner in faith. We both realized that we'd been blessed in finding each other, and that some Higher Power had to be involved not only in our lives but in all of what exists. *Had God been the source of power that turned my life around?* I wondered. I began reading the Bible regularly at the treatment center, and it became a part of my daily routine. The more I read, the more I felt a void that needed to be filled.

My stay at Betty Ford was a life-altering experience. After my stint there, I lost all desire for alcohol. That made me an anomaly, from what I'd heard during my group sessions. I felt I had been cured, although I accepted the fact that I would always be a recovering alcoholic. My thirst for alcohol was being replaced by a thirst for knowledge about faith and God.

Still, I was often reminded that I would carry the baggage of my alcoholic past for this new journey. On the day that I was released from the Betty Ford Clinic, I got an ice cream cone to enjoy while I waited for my flight to depart the airport in Palm Springs. I was savoring my freedom and contemplating my experiences in the clinic when a guy walked up and looked at me with something just short of disgust.

"You're Pat Summerall, aren't you? Do you think CBS will let an old drunk back on the air?"

With that he walked off, leaving me to wonder what I'd ever done to him, and what I was going to do if his sentiments were widely held. *Is this how it is going to be from now on?* I wondered. His words seemed intended to hurt me, but in reality, they stirred my competitive instincts and made me all the more determined to prove the cynics wrong. It wasn't the first time that I used someone's negative comments as motivation for doing something positive.

A few weeks later, I found myself staring into the bathroom mirror late one night. The ravages of addiction and illness that had haunted me in that eerie early morning in Augusta just prior to the intervention were no longer there. A much rosier, happier face—a sober face—stared back at me for the first time in a very long time. But something still mystified me about that hungover morning in Georgia. I couldn't help but wonder how those lights kept getting brighter and brighter when I saw the frightening sight of what I had become. The same lights seemed perfectly normal the previous evening before I went out. If I hadn't seen what alcohol was doing to me in full light, I may have never consented to go to the Betty Ford Center.

Not long after my recovery and release from the clinic, I spoke to a group at a Dallas luncheon at SMU about my experiences, including that awful moment of truth in front of the mirror. Dallas Cowboys owner Jerry Jones came up to me afterward, and in the course of our conversation said, "I felt like you were talking to me." After Jerry walked away, I turned to see a set of very intense blue eyes fixed on me—those of my friend and former coach, Tom Landry.

"Pat, would you like to know why the lights got so bright?"

"I sure would, coach. I sure would."

"God sent the angels so you could get a good look at yourself. And they brightened the lights so you could see yourself in the mirror."

I learned a long time ago never to doubt the wisdom of Tom Landry.

CHAPTER TEN

SAVING A FRIEND

My Betty Ford Clinic counselors told me that once I was committed to sobriety, I would have to stop associating with my old drinking friends. They predicted that most would abandon me anyway, rather than be around someone who no longer shared their love of booze.

In fact, most of my good friends hung in there with me. Some made a point to check on my choice of beverages at social gatherings and ceremonies—which didn't offend me in the least. Even Jack Nicklaus, who has been known to correct my golf swing, my golf stance, and my choice of golf pants, took to walking up, peering into my drink glass, and inquiring, "Whatcha drinking, Pat?"

Actually, there has only been one time when I had any inclination to have a drink. It was a very low-key, spur of the moment thing. I went to pick up some barbecue at a restaurant to bring it home. It wasn't ready when I got there, so I took a seat. I got a whiff of barbecue and beer from a tray that went by, and the thought hit me: *It would be good to have a beer and a sandwich.*

That notion passed quickly, and I've never had another urge.

MY FRIEND MICK

One of the best things to come of my sobriety and the Betty Ford experience was that it actually brought me closer to another old buddy, Mickey Mantle, and—even better—it inspired him to seek help for his own severe alcoholism. The treatment gave Mickey more than a clear mind. It gave him some time to make peace with the world. Sadly, that period of peace ended all too soon for him.

Patients at the Betty Ford Center are not allowed outside contact except for ten minutes on Saturdays. Oddly, once he got into the program, Mickey used his ten minutes to call me.

"Did you have any fun when you were here, Pat?" he asked.

He sounded grim. I was afraid he was pining for a drink.

"No, Mickey, that's not what you're there for," I told him.

Silence. There was some great struggle going on within him. I could hear it in his gravelly voice when he finally spoke again. "Pat, when I get out of here I want you to promise me that if you ever see me take another drink, you'll kill me," he said.

I said that I couldn't promise, because it was in the hands of a greater power.

LOCKER-ROOM BUDDIES

When I was playing for the New York Giants, I got to know many of the Yankees, who shared our stadium and locker room. Most of the Yanks also stayed at the Concourse Plaza, where we were living, so we were neighbors for a few months each year. We even swapped dishes. I used pitcher Bob Turley's plates and cups during the football season.

It wasn't unusual for me to go out with Giants teammates and meet up with several Yankees for dinner and drinks. Sometimes we were joined by my locker mate, Mickey Mantle, and his close cronies Whitey Ford and Billy Martin—a guy whose rabble-rousing and heavy drinking were such a bad influence on Mickey that the Yanks once traded him away.

Mickey was a contradiction. He was shy with strangers, but once he got to know you, he was completely uninhibited. He did not like to speak in public and he was quiet around unfamiliar people. Around his friends, however, he would say whatever—and I do mean whatever—was on his mind. Over the years, our relationship slowly progressed from acquaintances to a great friendship. It was run through the ring of fire—or, more appropriately, the mouth of a bottle.

Mickey retired from the Yankees the same year I left the Giants. In the early years of my broadcasting career, I ran into him only occasionally. I spent a little more time with him once he opened his hot spot, Mickey Mantle's Restaurant and Sports Bar on Central Park South in 1988. Then, when I moved to the Dallas area in 1992, I found that Mickey had a home in Dallas, too. We became golfing buddies and socialized more and more. Mickey was unique among celebrities in that his fame as an athlete seemed to grow after his retirement. His memorabilia was the most prized of almost any ballplayer, and that put a lot of predatory autograph seekers and others on his trail.

A LOT IN COMMON

Since we had a long history—dating back to when I played minor league baseball with his twin brothers—he felt I was one of the few people he could trust. I found him to be a magnetic, contradictory sort of guy. He could be astonishingly crude and ruthlessly blunt, yet he had a kind heart and a wonderful sense of humor.

We had more in common than drinking problems. We'd both grown up in small rural towns, and we'd had troubled relationships with our fathers, though Mickey loved his domineering dad while I never developed any affection for my mostly absent one. Oddly enough, we'd also both suffered from serious leg problems when we were young but somehow managed to become professional athletes.

Mickey had been kicked in the leg during a high-school football game, and the injury developed into an inflammatory bone infection called osteomyelitis. Doctors considered amputation, but Mickey's mother refused. She had him transferred to a hospital in Oklahoma City, where he was treated with the new drug penicillin.

While he had blinding speed when he first came up to the majors, Mickey's leg problems never totally went away. They were compounded by his knee injuries, which started when he caught his spikes in a drainpipe covering in right field during the second game of the 1951 World Series as he was chasing Willie Mays's fly ball. Centerfielder Joe DiMaggio waved Mickey off the ball, but when Mickey turned away he planted his spikes in the drainpipe cover and tore ligaments in his right knee. After that, he played in pain the rest of his career. He had four knee operations, not to mention a hip infection, a torn thigh muscle, broken bones in his left and right feet, and bone chips in his shoulder.

FAMILY CURSE

There were a lot of stories about the Mantle "family curse," and how Mickey spent much of his life fearing a premature death from Hodgkin's disease, which had taken his father, "Mutt," and his two uncles before the age of forty. There's no question that one of the biggest heartaches of Mickey's life was losing his dad so early, and Mickey often talked about the fact that his father never got to see him play at the height of his career. Some said that's why he drank so heavily. He didn't do much to dispel that notion when he said, while in his midforties, "If I knew I was going to live this long, I would have taken better care of myself."

Still, Mickey told me that he felt his father, whose real name was Elvin, had smoked himself to death. "I can always remember my dad with a cigarette in his mouth . . . and a pack of cigarettes rolled up in the sleeves of his T-shirt," Mickey said.

Mutt also spent many years working in the zinc mines in Oklahoma, which also didn't help his health. Mickey never developed Hodgkin's, but his youngest son, Billy, who was named after Billy Martin, died of a Hodgkin's-related heart attack in 1994 at age thirty-six. I knew it tore at Mickey's insides. Mickey's sons Danny and David were healthy, but Mickey Jr. died of melanoma in 2000. Mickey was not around to grieve that loss.

ATHLETIC PROWESS

It was odd that health problems were so prevalent in this family of strong, athletic men. As a Yankee, Mickey was legendary for his speed and power. He slammed one home run around six hundred feet and hit another at Yankee Stadium that might have measured seven hundred feet or more had the ball not struck the very top of the right-field façade while it was still on the rise.

Mickey's power did not diminish with his retirement. Even in his sixties, Mickey could knock the cover off a golf ball. Playing with him at Preston Trail Golf Club in Dallas, I saw Mickey drive the ball over the green at the 370-yard seventeenth hole, and his shoulder was bothering him that day.

Mickey's poor putting kept him from being an outstanding golfer, but he always finished strong at the "nineteenth hole." I took to referring to him as "my competitive drinking buddy," and we matched each other drink for drink after our round. We drank until we couldn't stand up, and sometimes we drank until we couldn't sit up. Mickey loved any kind of competition, whether it was matching me whiskey for whiskey—his favorite poison—playing golf, or gambling. Mickey loved to wager on sports, especially football. He bet a pile of money on the college games each Saturday, and usually had to hustle on Sunday to try to make up for lost ground with the pro teams.

He called me once during football season and asked where I was going to be broadcasting that weekend. I told him I'd be in Kansas City, covering a game at Arrowhead Stadium. He said, "I may call you. It depends on how I do on Saturday with the college games." Sure enough, the phone rang in my Kansas City hotel room early Sunday morning.

"The colleges killed me, Pat," he said. "I'm down about $3,500. I need some sure things in the pros."

I was pretty plugged in to the league, so I gave him three games that I thought looked pretty promising. All three of them hit. Giving those tips to Mickey was a big mistake. From then on, no matter what city I was in, he would track me down in my hotel Sunday morning and call me: "What do you think today, Pat?"

Mickey was a hard guy to say no to.

A PRIVATE MAN

Although Mickey learned to live with an unusual level of fame, he preferred to be treated like a regular guy, which meant being left alone. Even in the days before sports memorabilia became a fanatic's pursuit, people wanting his autograph or his investment in a business venture hounded Mickey night and day.

He was usually gracious to fans when they stopped him on the street. He carried a stack of autographed postcard-sized pictures with him, which he'd hand out and make a quick getaway before a crowd formed. But if he felt trapped in a crowd, he could get mean. Once we were on a private motor coach together, and word got out he was there. Somehow a bunch of people finagled their way on the bus, and they were really crowding him. He got upset and cussed some of them. He couldn't stand to be pressed.

SMALL-TOWN STAR

Mickey was born in Spavinaw, Oklahoma, and grew up in nearby Commerce, both of them tiny rural towns. He always considered himself a small-town guy, and he didn't pretend to be anything else. He started playing baseball professionally at the age of nineteen, so he never had the opportunity to polish his vocabulary or to develop a more sophisticated view of the world. He was unpretentious, and people sometimes made the mistake of thinking he wasn't very bright. He was smart enough, but not worldly in any way. So it threw him off to be treated like royalty in big cities, especially in New York, where he was worshiped.

Once we were both at the Regency hotel in Manhattan, and we had agreed to meet at a favorite restaurant just behind it. I made the mistake of walking out the front of the hotel, where photographers, autograph seekers, and other people were milling around looking for Mickey. It took me awhile to push through the crowd and finally get to the restaurant around back. Mickey wasn't there yet. I figured he got caught up in the throng. But a few minutes later he walked in with a lady friend, completely calm and unruffled; he'd sneaked out a back door.

"Good. A million people were in the lobby. You'd still be there," I said.

"Yeah, you mean those paraplegics?" he said.

"Gee, I don't know, Mick," I said, startled that Mickey would say such a thing. "I didn't see anybody in a wheelchair."

Mickey didn't hear me. Instead he kept going on about "those paraplegics," saying that he'd gotten one "with a real good elbow—knocked the @%!& out of him."

Now, I knew Mickey didn't like to be crowded. But I couldn't imagine him elbowing a guy in a wheelchair. Seeing my confusion, Mickey's long-time lady friend, Greer Johnson, stopped me short: "No, no, no. He doesn't mean he hit a paraplegic. He means *paparazzi!*" she said.

GETTING CLEAN

After I went through the Betty Ford Center for my alcohol addiction, Mickey began to realize that he had to do something about his drinking, too. I sensed he really wanted to address it, but he didn't know how

He was shy at first about broaching the subject, but as time passed he asked me more and more questions about the program and what I thought of it.

"Are they big into religion out there?" he asked.

"Well, yeah—it's part of it," I answered.

I asked him what denomination he was.

"What's that?"

"Are you a Baptist or Methodist or Presbyterian . . . ?"

"I ain't never been to church."

"Well, being from Oklahoma, you probably are a Baptist," I told him.

"That'll be fine," he said. "I'll take that."

Finally, in December of 1993, Mickey decided he would enter rehab, but not without a few assurances. He said he'd do the twenty-eight day program. "But I ain't goin' if they don't count weekends," he said.

I called the center to see if they had a bed, and I even got them to agree to count the weekend days for Mickey if that's what it was going to take to get him there and get him sober. Grudgingly Mickey went, entering a few days after Christmas.

A few months after Mickey got out, his son Billy died. I was concerned about Mickey's mental well-being, and how the loss might affect his ability to stay sober. He called one morning just after I'd left for the golf course. Cheri answered.

"Burnsie! How ya doing?" he said. It was his nickname for her, taken from her maiden name, Burns.

His voice sounded slurred; Cheri feared that he'd hit the bottle because of the stress.

"Where's Patrick? I gotta have help," he said, sounding pathetic.

"He's golfing, Mickey. What on earth is wrong?"

"I been in an accident," he said.

Cheri asked him where he was.

"I'm in jail," Mickey explained.

He said he'd hit a truck carrying Mexican migrant workers.

"Burnsie, please help me," he said.

"Let me talk to the police officer," Cheri said.

"I can't. He's a Mexican, too."

"Mickey, you're drunk!" she said.

"Oh, Burnsie. April Fools!"

Mickey obviously hadn't lost his sense of humor, despite all of his troubles. He was sober, and, we later learned, he'd been up since early morning making similar prank calls to friends across the country. We should have known. Mickey loved April Fool's Day pranks.

SOBER FRIENDS

To my knowledge, Mickey never took another drink after he completed the Betty Ford program. One night we reunited at our favorite Italian restaurant in Manhattan, the Capriccio behind the Regency. We'd been going there to eat for thirty years, usually after many hours at surrounding watering holes.

This time when we came through the doors, sober for perhaps the first time, the staff knew not to set us up with the usual drinks. But once we sat down, the owner did send over a plate of calamari, which we'd always had as an appetizer. Mickey was telling a story when the calamari arrived. As he talked, he grabbed a piece and flipped it into his mouth.

He then got this terrible, disgusted look on his face and spit the calamari out into his napkin. "What is that?" he said.

"Mick, that's the same calamari we've been eating for years," I said.

"Yeah? Well, I could never taste that @%!& before!" he said.

SEEKING PEACE

Mickey seemed to cherish the simpler life and the quiet times we spent together, especially when we were playing golf and hanging out at his condominium on Lake Oconee in southern Georgia. Residents of the town had embraced him, and they made an informal pact to treat Mickey like just another neighbor, which he appreciated. They even refused to point out his house to strangers, who might be reporters or sports memorabilia fanatics.

Still, his fame continued to dog Mickey even in those days. We were both at our homes outside Dallas when he called one day in 1995 to say that he wanted to get some peace and quiet. Apparently, autograph seekers were bothering him even at home. We were headed out of town on a trip, so I offered to let him use our house in Colleyville—a quiet suburb of Dallas—as a hideout. "Just come to our house," I told him. "Nobody will know you're here, and nobody will bother you."

"You're kidding," he said.

I insisted that it was a sincere invitation.

Mickey accepted. He stayed at our house for several days, and later told me that he appreciated it more than I understood.

"That's the nicest thing anybody's ever done for me. I mean, you gave me the run of your house!"

His gratitude made me realize that it is possible to be lonely even when millions of people know your name and want to be around you. In truth, Mickey had very few friends he could trust.

FRIEND IN NEED

Though he'd quit drinking, Mickey's health deteriorated and he was losing weight rapidly. Months after his treatment, he insisted I meet him at Preston Trail Golf Club in Dallas to show me something important.

It took me an hour to get there, and I was worried about him as I made the drive. The clubhouse was all but empty when I got there. Mickey and an attendant were in the locker room.

I asked what it was he wanted me to see about.

With that, he turned away from me and pulled his shorts down. "Look at my butt, Pat. I used to have a great looking butt. Now look at it!"

"Mickey, is that what you called me all the way over here for—just to look at your butt?"

"I wanted you to see how terrible it is," he said.

Cheri was right. I had some strange friends.

But in this case, I decided Mickey wasn't just messing with me. He was distraught about his declining health. His liver was severely damaged from years of heavy drinking. He also suffered from a once-dormant hepatitis C infection he'd gotten from a transfusion during a knee surgery. Mickey was getting sicker and sicker. I encouraged him to see a doctor.

FINAL INNINGS

In early 1995, Mickey was diagnosed with liver cancer. He was admitted to Baylor University Medical Center in late May of that year and then approved to get on a transplant list. He received a successful liver transplant just a day after the release of the first media reports of his approval for a transplant.

Some people howled that Mickey got favored treatment; people often wait for months to get a transplant. But the truth is, he qualified for it. He had been sober for more than six months, was a very sick man, and had Type O blood, the most common. He got the transplant because he was the perfect candidate.

Unfortunately, the transplant did not restore Mickey's health. In early August, doctors found that cancer had moved into Mickey's lungs and other parts of his body. Antirejection drugs for the transplanted liver apparently weakened his immune system, making it easier for the cancer to spread. On August 13, 1995, my dear friend died at Baylor University Medical Center in Dallas, less than two months after receiving the transplant.

The world mourned the loss of one of its greatest athletes, and I mourned the loss of a great, loyal friend. But I was glad for one thing that happened to Mickey after he became sober. Despite his lack of experience with organized religion, Mickey found faith. The things he learned at the Betty Ford Center and from visits from his old Yankee teammate Bobby Richardson led him to God. He was baptized and seemed to gain fresh wisdom as well as peace. In his last press conference, which he gave at the Ford Center, Mickey said he was no hero: "God gave me everything, and I blew it. For the kids out there, don't be like me!"

He also kept his sense of humor to the end. At the press conference, he recognized renowned Mantle memorabilia collector Barry Halper in the crowd, and took the opportunity to give him a teasing jab: "Barry, what did you pay for my old liver?"

Later, I wished I'd put in a bid for it myself.

CHAPTER ELEVEN

AMAZING GRACE

I STOOD IN WHITE ROBES BEFORE GOD AND EVERYONE—A SIXTY-SIX-year-old man waiting to be immersed in a baptismal pool. A coterie of five- and six-year-olds were dancing at my knees. Four years after my thirty-three day stint at the Betty Ford Center in 1992, I hadn't had another taste of alcohol. I had left that life for another.

The Betty Ford treatment was amazingly effective, but the impact reached much deeper than my addiction to alcohol. It also inspired my curiosity about God and an awakening of faith that found me center stage for a Sunday service at the First Baptist Church in Euless, Texas. I felt vulnerable and embarrassed, but mostly excited. I was a man among boys—well, a grandfather among mere kids. Yet we were sharing a very important day, our baptism. In more ways than one, I was taking a plunge.

A NEW THIRST

My reliance on the bottle had been replaced by a healthier thirst—one for knowledge about Christianity and the Holy Bible. I was experiencing a vastly different level of awareness. Each morning, I awoke with a clear head. For that, I'd say a prayer of thanks and then I would ask God's guid-ance. I'd abandoned the hedonistic lifestyle for one of physical and spiri-tual transformation. And Cheri walked the walk with me. We began attending church every Sunday as a couple. She listened each morning as I read aloud from the Bible and other devotional books. Our lives had changed immeasurably for the better.

It was a big help to me that Cheri quit drinking at the same time, even though she had always been a very controlled social drinker. She had tried to get me to stop drinking, and when I entered the clinic after the intervention I could tell she was relieved. She came to see me a couple of times at Betty Ford, but only during limited visiting hours. I think it brought us closer together because we became more focused on each other once I gave up drinking.

Our pastor, Dr. Claude Thomas, visited our house one night, and the conversation turned to the significance and symbolism of baptism. I'd been baptized as a baby, but only recently had my faith taken on a more personal meaning. So I asked Dr. Thomas if he'd do the honors this time around, and he graciously agreed. When the day came I felt an odd sense of helplessness, standing before the baptismal, awaiting my turn to go under, watching this small-framed man of God baptize the kids, worry-ing that he might not be able to pull me back up and out of the water once I was submerged. Talk about an act of faith!

I took my place and I crossed my arms, preparing to slide under the water. I was oblivious to the pastor's introduction of me before the con-gregation. I felt a light push and down I went. But I came up almost as fast—in the sure hands of the pastor, who had no problem pulling me back up. When I did reemerge, it was as though I had surfaced to a new world. I can only describe that moment as the sensation of being born. In fact, for the first time in my life, I knew what people meant about being "born again." I had already accepted that Jesus Christ was the Son of God who died for our sins. Now, I felt I was truly part of his family. I felt ecstatic, invigorated, happier, and freer. It felt as though my soul had been washed clean.

It may sound corny, but since then I've never been cold; I have a warm feeling that has never left me, no matter how cold it might be outside. I may need a coat, but I never get cold even during games in Green Bay. It is the strangest sensation. I attribute it to the baptism and being reborn.

During the baptism, that sense of comfort came over me and it has never left. I interpret it as God's love, the blanket of warmth that seems to surround me. It's a sense of security, satisfaction, and contentment with where I am. I feel better about my relationship with God than ever before.

NEWFOUND FAITH

In all of those years as a football player and broadcaster, I had vainly thought I was in control of everything in my life, but I wasn't. God was— and is. All I had to do to build a relationship with him was to invite him in. Finally, I had. There is a Savior—there is a God, I realized. And if he would have me, I'd love him for the rest of my life.

My lifelong sense of hope—that confident anticipation of good that sustained me through the years—finally had its perfect complement: a newfound and enduring faith. It had been the missing ingredient in my world all those years, a void I had often filled with alcohol and fast living. Now I revel in the redeeming grace that God has bestowed upon me. And for the first time, I realized how closely linked the virtues of hope and faith truly are.

The apostle Peter urges us in the Bible to rest our hope "fully upon the grace that is to be brought to you at the revelation of Jesus Christ." I strongly felt that I was doing just that.

After my baptism, I found myself often reflecting and identifying with the classic gospel song "Amazing Grace," particularly the familiar line that goes: "How sweet the sound that saved a wretch like me. I once was lost, but now am found. Was blind, but now I see." Cheri and I named our home in Southlake, Texas, "Amazing Grace," and our black Labrador retriever is "Gracie."

WALKING THE TALK

As the months and years of sobriety passed, I began to speak openly about my transformation to others who could benefit from my experience. I wanted them to know the depth of my faith. Obviously, I no longer think of Christian men as weak. I know the strength it takes to live a Christian life. I've seen the other side.

When I'm invited to speak, the audience often wants to hear about that "other side" of my life. So I entertain them with stories from my life in sports, but I always make sure I leave them with my testimony about the pitfalls of a life without faith, and the amazing grace that comes with being a strong Christian.

I do not pretend—in my speeches or elsewhere—to be the model of a perfect Christian, however. I struggle with it every day. The thing I have had the most difficulty with is forgiveness. I really have to work on it, and I'm proud of my successes. Forgiving and forgetting is a tough thing for me to do. I've had some business dealings with partners that went sour, and I had to work on forgiving them, but I did.

One former broadcast coworker wrote in a book that I had once disparaged one of my favorite places in the world, Augusta National; it took me a long time to heal the wounds from that lie. Ken Venturi used to quote the Italian saying, "Don't get mad, get even." It's tempting to follow that, but there is no peace in it. Revenge only eats you up.

PRAY TO FORGIVE

The subject of forgiveness has also been one of the many topics my grown children and I have discussed. I have asked them to forgive me for my failings as a husband to their mother and as a father to them. It has taken them a long time to find the will and the strength to do that. I certainly understand. Kathy's death triggered powerful emotions, including anger and resentment toward me. They were all very close to Kathy, and I was not there for them. We talked it through in depth, and, with God's help, we came through it closer than before because they found the strength to forgive me to a greater degree than they had before. I still have much to make up. It will take a lot of prayer.

There are many ways to pray. I often do mine while driving in the car. I like to talk to God. I think of it as me and God in the booth. It's not the same as talking to Madden or Jack Buck or Brookie in the booth, but in some ways, it is similar. I know that my voice carries a lot farther in conversations with God. I always liked what former Washington Redskins coach Joe Gibbs said about his prayer methods. (He won three Super Bowls with three different quarterbacks, so he obviously knew the power of prayer.) A strong Christian, Joe said that when he goes to bed at night, he throws his shoes far enough under the bed so that in the morning, he has to get down on his knees to get them out.

"And while I'm down there, I pray," he said.

NEW LIFE

I had been doing TV for about thirty years before my intervention, and during that time I had partied with increasing intensity behind the scenes. Through all those decades, viewers remained loyal to me, and to the men who partnered with me. My fans were apparently responding to something that they picked up at both an audio and visual level. One of my big concerns while going through the treatment was, what if sober Pat Summerall no longer projects that confidence or indefinable quality? What if those same viewers stop responding to me?

It's funny, because I didn't broach that subject with my counselor, Tom Martin, at Betty Ford. Tom came up with it on his own one day during our session. He had seen professional pilots, lawyers, and entertainers express similar concerns, wondering if being sober would somehow hinder them or change their professional personas.

Tom asked me if such thoughts were bothering me.

"Exactly," I had told him.

Tom replied that he couldn't promise me that being sober would not affect my work adversely, but he gently reminded me that viewers can't respond at all to a broadcaster who is dead.

Once I left the Betty Ford Center, I returned to broadcasting. I was happy to discover there were no bad side effects from having a clear head and no hangover. I rejoined John after my rehab, and it went without a hitch. Like many people who've shed the burden of drinking, I felt re-energized. My life took on new purpose. I wanted to share the story of my recovery and my renewal of faith with others as a way of paying back those who had cared enough to stop my downward spiral. I gave many speeches and interviews, but I wanted to do something more in depth.

I contacted Dallas literary agent Jan Miller, who has many high-profile clients, and she put me on course to do a book. We put together a proposal and set up a series of meeting in New York City to talk to the publishers who expressed an interest in my story.

I had to be in Philadelphia on September 9, and we had to drive to New York City for the Giants-Packers game the next week for Fox with John. Cheri came along because we had theater tickets and a room at the Regency hotel, our favorite. That night we had dinner with NFL Commissioner Paul Tagliabue and his wife, Chan, at their apartment on Park Avenue.

On Tuesday, the eleventh, Jan and I met and headed for the landmark Flatiron Building at Fifth Avenue and Broadway for our first meeting. We'd just sat down in a conference room when someone ran past and shouted that a plane had struck the World Trade Center, less than three miles away. It was very odd because as Cheri and I had entered the city, we'd talked about those same twin towers, how striking they were and how she'd once dined at Windows on the World at the top.

Jan and I went to the windows on the south side of the Flatiron Building, where we could see a huge, smoking hole in the North Tower. Someone speculated that a police helicopter had lost control and slammed into the building. But that didn't sound right. I looked at the size of the opening and said to Jan, "To make a hole like that, it had to be something much, much bigger."

About that time, I noticed a large passenger jet approaching us from across the Hudson River. I thought it must be headed for La Guardia Airport. I quickly realized, however, that it was flying far too fast to land there. From my vantage point, it didn't appear to be on a trajectory to hit anywhere near us, but then it seemed to disappear inside the south tower of the World Trade Center. A few seconds later—although it seemed like a much longer time—we saw flames shoot out of the other side.

I had the same stunned sense of fear, sorrow, and dread that I'd experienced upon learning that President Kennedy had been shot and killed decades earlier. But this was a much more massive and violent attack—and it was close enough to pose a physical threat. Obviously, many lives were lost—and were still in danger—at that moment. Jan and I made a unanimous decision to get out of there as quickly as possible.

By the time we got down the elevator and to the street, both the north and south towers had given way and collapsed. Smoke, soot, and debris were already clouding the air. Fortunately, we'd arranged for a driver to wait for us. To his credit, he had stayed put during all the tumult. As we got in the car and moved away, we heard the horrifying reports on the radio. We passed groups of people huddled together, praying on the side-walks. Others hurried up Broadway, trying to make calls on their cell phones. Crowds gathered around television sets in storefronts.

It took us a very long time to go those few miles to Jan's apartment—probably more than an hour. After she got out, the driver turned to me and said that he desperately needed to get home to his family in Long Island. I said, "Okay, go ahead. I'll walk the rest of the way to the hotel." Traffic was at a standstill, so I figured I'd probably make better time on foot while he tried to get home to his loved ones.

It was eerie. I knew that, just a few blocks away, many were dying and suffering. No one could be sure that the attacks were over. No one knew if other planes were coming, if other buildings had been targeted, or if bombs had been planted. There were all sorts of scary rumors. It was disorienting to walk down such familiar streets with so many people dis-traught and unsure what to do. Time seemed to move in stops and starts. It took me at least two hours to get back to my hotel, but it seemed like minutes.

Just as I walked in the entrance to the Regency, an announcement came over the hotel P.A. system: "Stand by to evacuate the hotel."

"Why are we evacuating this hotel? We're a long way away from the World Trade Center," I asked the concierge.

He told me that the Israeli delegation to the United Nations was in our hotel, and there were concerns that they might be targeted, too.

I hurried upstairs to our room and found Cheri still there. I had not been able to reach her, so she was upset. She had no idea where I had been during the attack. Fortunately, the hotel decided not to evacuate after all, so we had time to make our plans to get out of town. I managed to get a call through to Dallas sports broadcaster Norm Hitzges, for whom I did a regular NFL report, and we did a long and intense segment on the air about what I'd experienced.

John Madden also has an apartment in Manhattan, and we'd been talking on and off by cell phone about the terrorist attack and its far-reaching effects. We were pretty certain that the game would be cancelled, but we had not received official word. We didn't get it until two days later, but at that point getting out of New York was still a serious challenge.

All the airports were shut down and the bridges and tunnels out of the city were still closed, though we heard they might open again by Thursday. The emotional intensity started to get to me by Wednesday evening. I don't know that I've ever been through a time of such uncertainty about the security of our country and its stability. I had to get out and air out my brain. Cabin fever had set in, even though we were in a Park Avenue hotel and hardly suffering. Cheri and I decided to walk down to St. Patrick's Cathedral, which is always a comforting presence amid the chaos of Manhattan. But as we started our walk of nearly a mile down there, it hit us that there was no chaos. As we turned on to Fifth Avenue near the Presbyterian Church, we were amazed to see that it was all but deserted of civilians. No traffic. No throngs of people. None of the typical Manhattan mayhem. The only human beings in sight were soldiers in full combat mode, patrolling the streets with rifles while roaring fighter jets crossed the skies overhead.

The only sound from the streets was an eerie wail coming from the steps of the church. There, a lone trumpeter stood playing "God Bless, America" over and over and over. The familiar song took on new meaning in that oddly cinematic setting, eerily devoid of the usual mobs, and with the presence of the soldiers and the military jets lending to our discomfiting sense of vulnerability. The song would never sound the same again to me. The trumpeter's solemn notes followed us for several blocks, resonating off the empty streets and buildings. There are times when I can still hear it reverberating through the manmade canyons of Manhattan, and it gives me no comfort.

Cheri and I grew increasingly anxious to get out of New York. We decided to try to rent a car and drive west—perhaps to Cincinnati, where we could then catch a flight home. Of course, finding a rental car was itself a challenge. Everyone wanted out of New York, or so it seemed. After hours on the phone Thursday morning, we caught a break. A Hertz representative who took my call was a New York Giants fan who remembered my playing days. He said he would hold a car for me if I could get there in twenty minutes. I took off walking—there were no cabs to be found—to the Hertz office.

At the Hertz office, we finally secured the car—thanks to that Giants fan—and headed back to the hotel. "Start packing," I told Cheri. We just threw everything together and loaded up the car; all the bellhops and staff were telling us to be careful—we'd come together like a family during a crisis.

The next morning, we began a 1,600-mile journey back home. I had dreaded the trip, but it proved to be therapeutic. Everywhere we stopped there was a sense of shared concern; certainly there was no little fear, but it was also heartwarming to see people from all parts of the country pull together as Americans. It seemed like every car, every building, and every house we passed displayed an American flag or some other patriotic symbol.

After one particularly long stretch, we stopped at a gas station with an adjoining sandwich shop in West Virginia. Cheri hopped out to get us something to eat while I put gasoline in the car. A couple of guys parked in a pickup truck appeared to recognize me. One of them approached and in a thick Southern drawl asked what I was doing there.

I told him I was driving home to Dallas.

He guessed that I had been in New York City but teased that "I thought somebody sent you down here to teach us all how to talk."

I didn't think it was the time to tell him that I, too, was a country boy, so I assured him that I was just trying to get home, offered him a "God bless," and pointed the car down the road.

Near Nashville, we heard on the car radio that air traffic was resuming, so we made a beeline to the airport. We got seats aboard a Delta flight to Dallas that was supposed to leave within an hour but because of security concerns it turned out to be a five-hour wait. There were only five people on our plane. Before we took off, the captain came back to the seating area and talked to each one of the passengers, assuring them that the plane was in very good hands. Much had changed in those few days, and much would never be the same again.

A HIGHER CALLING

John Madden and I worked through the 2001–2002 football season together, enjoying it all the way through the dramatic Super Bowl XXXVI. John's plans were set. He would be joining the crew for *Monday Night Football*. I briefly contemplated retirement until Fox recruited me for the 2002–2003 football season. They teamed me with broadcaster Brian Baldinger for seventeen games—including ten with the Cowboys.

It proved to be a dismal season for Dallas. I did some traveling with the team, and sometimes talked football with owner Jerry Jones. After one particularly bad game, Jerry handed me a legal pad.

"Pat, I want you to write down everything that I've done wrong with the Cowboys and what I need to do to correct the situation," he said.

"Jerry, if I do that, you will never speak to me again."

He insisted. But rather than kick a team owner when he was down, I picked up the pen and pad and wrote three words of advice: "Hire Bill Parcells."

A few weeks later, I was in Washington in a production meeting for the final Cowboys game when Jerry Jones asked to talk to me immediately. He called me out into the hall. He was very excited.

"Okay, Pat, I got Parcells for four years, and he says he's gonna turn this thing around," Jones said. "And Pat, what that means is *you* better stay for four more years."

I couldn't make that promise, but it was very nice to know that I was still appreciated, and that I could still contribute to the game that has given me so much. In truth, however, I had begun to feel called to talk less about football and more about my addiction and rebirth. John Weber, the Dallas Cowboys' chaplain, presented me with such an opportunity. John asked me to speak at his alma mater, Dakota Wesleyan University in Mitchell, South Dakota. It was a small school in a small town, but I reaped big rewards that night.

Several hundred people filled the college gym, and were an attentive and respectful audience. I never considered myself an evangelist or revivalist; it's just not my thing. But I felt inspired that night as I shared my story with them, especially when I told them about my rebirth as a Christian. Suddenly—one after another—men, women, and young people came forward and told me that they, too, had accepted Christ. Nearly a hundred of them lined up in front of the stage. It was better than booting a fifty-yard field goal or calling a Super Bowl touchdown. For that one night in South Dakota, I felt like Billy Graham!

CHAPTER TWELVE

FAITH PREVAILS

Most former professional football players hobble quietly into the night. As a competitor for twenty years, I was hobbling until I underwent knee-replacement surgery in 2000. The surgery went well and my recovery was swift, but there is one aspect of knee-replacement surgery that stays with you and cannot be neglected.

A year later, I felt a sharp pain during an NFL play-by-play broadcast. Oddly enough, the pain was in my mouth. I saw a dentist the next day; he found a minor problem with a tooth and fixed it. The same day, I jumped back on a plane to call another regular-season game on the weekend before Christmas. No one—not Cheri, not me, not the dentist—had given any thought to a crucial fact that my surgeons had warned us about repeatedly following my knee-replacement surgery: from that point forward, I needed to take antibiotics two hours before and two hours after I had any dental work. Bacteria, we were told, could easily enter the bloodstream during even the most routine dental procedure and lodge around the knee-replacement site. I'd forgotten all about that warning, and it was an oversight for which I would pay dearly.

Back home on Christmas Day, I awoke to a raging fever and a swollen knee. It finally sunk in what was happening, and Cheri took me to the hospital, where they found I had developed a massive knee infection. My knee was so overrun by bacteria that the doctor told Cheri my life could be endangered. The scary part was that doctors couldn't pinpoint the specific type of infection, so they had to dose me heavily with a broad-spectrum of antibiotics and hope for the best.

Thankfully, I'm a tough ol' coot. In a few days I was feeling good enough that I thought I could return to work. I hopped a plane for another game in another town, refusing to listen to my wife and doctors. After so many years, I was just wired to work. By the time I got home, I was dragging badly and I had to go back to the hospital. This time, doctors were able to isolate that pesky organism and hit me with massive doses of penicillin—the only thing that could contain such a stubborn infection. They knocked it down, but I struggled through the rest of the season and Super Bowl XXXVI—my final game with John Madden in 2002.

TOLL TAKEN

It took a few months for me to fully regain my strength after the season. Even then, my doctors were concerned. They felt my immune system had been compromised, which was dangerous because my body had taken some serious abuse. Our family physician, Dr. Paul Wade, told us that this sort of opportunistic infection could easily wreak havoc on my weakest major organs—in my case, the liver, which was in especially bad shape from all those years of heavy drinking.

I soldiered on through the next NFL season—my final tour with Fox—but I never felt quite right all year. I continued to suffer minor bleeds. In the spring of 2003, I felt good enough to fly to Los Angeles for a football-broadcasting seminar, while Cheri stayed behind with visiting family members. In L.A., I suffered another major bleed, and this one was exceptionally bad. I vomited blood almost uncontrollably. I went to the emergency room, where my vital signs were so poor I had to be carted up to intensive care, barely conscious. Cheri rushed out to L.A., not knowing whether I would be dead or alive when she got there.

By the time she arrived, a transfusion had improved my vitals and I had stabilized. My quality of life was diminishing rapidly, and my long-term prognosis was not good. I was on a slippery slope and losing traction. While we were in L.A., the doctor who was on duty performed a relatively new, minimially invasive banding procedure. He tied off several main veins in hopes that the blood would find a less-dangerous route and bypass my liver. After the procedure, I got better, but we realized this was only a Band-Aid approach. I had betrayed my liver with booze, and now it was breaking down.

BODY IN REVOLT

Your body's ammonia levels rise as the liver loses its ability to filter out toxins. If the levels get too high, it can kill you before the clogged liver shuts down. My ammonia levels ebbed and flowed dangerously. The results from my regular blood work were increasingly disturbing. Every day, it seemed, I saw a different somber doctor with his own deep concerns.

On the night before Thanksgiving Day in 2003, I got a major transfusion and I immediately felt much, much better—even well before the five-hour procedure was completed. My energy level was up again and I thought, *Well, this is better.* I enjoyed Thanksgiving dinner and even played a little golf over the holiday weekend.

On the following Monday, Paul took blood work again to see how well the transfusion was "holding." It wasn't. Paul saw the results and called Cheri immediately with the bad news. "What would normally last about three months has lasted only a few days," he told her. "The transfusion is not holding. It means his liver is very bad."

Just over a month later, in January 2004, there was more disturbing news. Paul got us both together for a conference call. My blood work, he said, was getting even worse. Despite more than eleven years of abstinence from alcohol, my liver was not healing. Paul delivered the news we had both feared—a liver transplant was the only likely solution to my condition.

We wasted no time getting to a liver specialist in Dallas, but my knee infection, my need for antibiotics, and my age made me a poor candidate for the surgery. "I'm just afraid nobody will transplant you," he said.

There was another mitigating factor—I was a celebrity. The brouhaha over Mickey Mantle's liver transplant had made many programs gun shy, especially Baylor University Medical Center, where Mickey's transplant was done.

"Baylor will never talk with you," the doctor said. "What happened with Mickey Mantle's transplant may be held against you. People thought he got favorable treatment."

REJECTED

It was a long drive home from that grim meeting. A million things were going through my mind. I needed to relax, so I decided to go ahead with a golf game I'd lined up a couple of days earlier. The way things were going, I didn't know how many more chances I might get to play. As I was donning my golf pants and golf shoes, trying to keep a stiff upper lip, Cheri walked into the room, crying.

"I feel like you've been handed a death sentence," she said. "And we can't do anything about it."

She grabbed my arm, looked me in the eye, and said, "Tell me what you're thinking."

Like most men, I didn't like dealing with emotions. I preferred confronting the facts and looking for solutions. "Cheri, I don't know how right now, but I am going to beat this thing. Mark my words, I am going to beat it."

I hugged her and headed out the door.

By February, golf—or just about any other kind of physical activity—was out of the question. I was still functioning, but I was exhausted. As my body grew more toxic, I slept more and more. On one Saturday night, I fell asleep and almost couldn't wake up.

Eleven hours. Twelve hours. Thirteen hours passed, and I was still out. By this point, Cheri was very worried. She burned up the phone lines with Dr. Paul. She kept telling him that something different was going on with me this time, but when he asked if I was coherent and making sense, she said that I was. He said as long as I was making sense she should let me sleep, but to make an appointment for Monday morning. I slept sixteen hours, got up, ate a little, and fell back into a deep sleep.

Somehow, Cheri was able to rouse me on Monday and get me dressed. When we got to the doctor's office, Paul took one look at me and called for an emergency team to cart me over to intensive care at Presbyterian Hospital, which fortunately was connected to his medical office building. Paul followed us over to the ICU. It wasn't long before he emerged from the unit and grimly told my wife that my ammonia levels were so dangerously high that there was a good chance I could pass away in the next few hours.

My body was poisoned, he said, and I probably couldn't endure much more.

"You'd better call the kids," he told Cheri.

I was in a deep, almost comatose state, unaware that Cheri called my grown children and they made arrangements to come. She held my hand, but I had no awareness of that or anything else. At one point, she later told me, she whispered, "Pat, if you need to go, don't hang on for me. I want you here more than anything, but I don't want you suffering."

Some time late in the afternoon, I came to, looked up at Cheri, and said, "What happened?"

She seemed surprised. She wasn't the only one.

CLOSE CALL

The kids got there that evening, expecting to see their dad on his death bed. Instead, I was sitting up, eating Jell-O, wondering *Why all the fuss.*

"What are you doing here? This really must be bad," I said to them.

Even my doctor was out of medical explanations. "Never count him out," he said, smiling. "Never count him out."

But when I fell asleep again, Paul herded my kids into a side room and explained the reality of my situation. "Your father may have rallied, but he is on his last legs," he said. "Without a transplant, it's just a matter of time . . ."

For the next few days and weeks, I teetered on the brink of death, alternating between pain and hope, consciousness and unconsciousness. During this time in the hospital, we heard from dozens of friends and fans. The outpouring was just amazing. My old booth mate John Madden called almost daily. We heard regularly from Jack Nicklaus, Tom Brookshier, and Bill Parcells, among many others. Bill said he was praying for me!

Imagine that, I thought. In our long association and friendship, I had never heard this craggy tough guy say he prayed for anybody. But Bill said it to me, and he said it to my wife, over and over. We were touched.

LOOKING BACK

My children, Susan, Kyle, and Jay, came to stay with Cheri in Southlake, so they could come to see me in the hospital. They had been coming to see us over the past four or five years, but this time they had been called to my death bed. It gave me cause to marvel once again at how well they had turned out as adults, mostly thanks to their mother, Kathy. It was a very difficult time for them because Kathy had been ill with cancer but was in remission from her rare form of abdominal cancer. At that point, she was remarkably well and she was determined to beat it, but doctors said her prognosis was grim.

After my football days, Kathy and I moved to Connecticut. I took over as the morning man at WCBS radio in New York, working seven days a week, month after month, broadcasting games almost every Saturday and Sunday—on top of my many weekday radio duties. The cycle repeated itself almost ceaselessly. I fell into a work pattern that may have boosted my career, but it took me out of their lives.

Breakfast was an important time at the house; it was about the only time I could keep up with the kids, except for maybe a few odd hours on the weekend. So the responsibility of raising the kids fell to Kathy, and she served them well as a strong Christian mother and a guiding influence. But every family will tell you that kids also need their father's influence, and my children rarely had that benefit.

As a young professional, I faced a dilemma that so many others face as they climb the career ladder. In the process of making a better life for my family, I neglected them. And as my professional world expanded, I stayed away longer on road trips and drank more to pass the time. And as heavy drinkers do, I did many irrational things. My children grew up without me, and I realized there was no recovering my lost time with them. When they became adults, we gathered occasionally, but my escalating drinking often put me at odds with them.

Though we loved one another, a gulf had grown between us that had really never been bridged. Susan, my oldest child—the one who wrote the painfully poignant letter that swayed my decision to go to Betty Ford—became a very successful mom and professional. She served as secretary to my old teammate Jack Kemp when he was a member of the House of Representatives. In recent years, trying to remain close to her own family, she has been serving as executive secretary to Jacksonville mayor John Peyton.

Jay became a successful businessman and in many ways assumed the role of family leader over the years. The others looked up to him. After graduating from the University of Florida, he went to work for the PGA Tour and two different tour commissioners, Dean Beman and Tim Finchem, before starting a career with AT&T and raising four kids. Jay now has his own company in the credit-card business and lives outside Philadelphia.

Kyle, like his dad, had his wild moments and was a little slower to mature than the others, but we reveled in the fact he had not only straightened his life out but he did so with passion, raising four kids and running a successful film production company that does commercials and documentaries. He's the only one of the gang who calls me "Pop."

There they were with me in what appeared to be my final days. I was ill and barely mobile, but I remained lucid most of the time. Our conversations were long, enjoyable, sometimes emotional—and very healing. In illness, the afflicted often call upon God, sometimes for the first time in their lives. But the longer my children spent around our home during my illness, the more they got the chance to see the kind of life I was leading, and how my sobriety, remarriage, and renewed faith had changed me for the better. Though my body was breaking down, they saw a spiritual renewal that they sensed was genuine. One day, I told Susan that I felt better about my relationship with God than ever before.

"That's the most powerful statement I've ever heard from you, that you feel good about your relationship with him," she said.

This time together, long overdue, was a great comfort to me—like the fulfillment of a final wish.

NEW HOPE

In mid-March our liver specialist in Dallas told us he had some good news and some bad news—and they were both the same. I was very close to qualifying for a liver transplant based on the extent of my liver disease. Unfortunately, I was not quite close enough. That meant I was in transplant limbo, and that it might serve me better to get just a little worse. Not a real attractive option. I didn't know how much worse I could get.

"I've done some research," the doctor said to us. "The most aggressive and best transplant center in the United States is the Mayo Clinic in Jacksonville, Florida. It's worth a try."

We contacted the staff at the Mayo Clinic in Jacksonville, which is only a few hours from Lake City. They agreed to let me come in for an evaluation. Cheri and I flew out to Jacksonville on March 16, our wedding anniversary. By this time I was incredibly bloated, having retained more than eighty pounds of fluid. I was growing increasingly uncomfortable every day and was not a happy traveler. To make matters worse, our plane was delayed for a very long time, first in the terminal and then on the runaway. I sat there, seriously afraid that I was going to burst.

Finally we landed in Jacksonville at just after 11:30 p.m., less than eight hours before the stressful evaluation was scheduled to start the next morning. The plane door opened, but we were forced to wait—again. The flight crew, it seemed, couldn't get the door into the terminal open. After a half-hour, the airline decided we'd have to disembark the old-fashioned way, on those rickety metal steps down to the tarmac.

Somehow, with the help of Cheri and the railing, I descended the steps very slowly, half sliding and half stepping down each rung, wearing slippers over my aching, bloated feet and drawstring pants over my bulging frame. The glamorous life of a network sportscaster seemed to belong to someone else, somewhere else in time.

A wheelchair courier met us at the bottom, and I collapsed into the chair. With the wind whipping through my hair and my entire body throbbing, I was pushed along the tarmac at midnight. I felt a hundred years old, trapped in the body twice my usual size.

WORTHINESS TESTED

The evaluation began early the next morning. The medical team mercilessly probed, prodded, pinned, and pulled, testing my heart, lung, and kidney functions. I knew they were just doing their job, but I vowed never to go through such torment again.

The team sensed my anguish. "We don't just give organs away," one of them explained to my wife. "If he is to receive this gift, he must be able to keep this gift."

Once I made it back to my hotel room, I took a warm bath and it struck me that I could barely see my toes. My feet and ankles had swollen even more, if that was possible, from all the fluid and toxins that my liver couldn't process. As I tried to raise myself out of the tub, something else occurred to me: I was stuck—really stuck—in the narrow bathtub. No matter what I did, I couldn't extricate my weakened body, which weighed more than three hundred pounds at this point.

Lord, what next? I struggled helplessly. The bath water was getting cool. I shivered, and finally called to Cheri for help. She came in but she couldn't budge me. Cheri finally called my son Kyle, who drove over from his office. He pulled me free. I'd been in the tub for hours. I was trembling from cold and embarrassment. One indignity piled upon another.

We were still hoping Methodist Hospital in Dallas would accept me, because I wasn't sure I'd be up to making another trip back out to Jacksonville. The Dallas doctors would accept Mayo's test results, we were told. On late Thursday I was released and cleared to travel back to Dallas. Cheri was trying to arrange for a flight on the hotel phone when her cell phone rang. It was Marilyn Love, Jerry Jones's secretary, calling from the Dallas Cowboys headquarters.

"Cheri, we know what's going on with Pat, so Jerry is sending his plane."

"What are you talking about, Marilyn?"

We had done everything possible to keep this a secret. We were afraid of triggering a backlash like that Mickey Mantle had faced. But word had leaked out around the Cowboys' camp.

"We know you're down at Mayo, and we know how sick Pat is. Jerry is sending his plane," Marilyn said sternly. "There is no discussion on this, Cheri. Do you want the plane tonight or in the morning?"

Stunned, Cheri said she'd have to call her back after checking with me. I was no help. I was so out of it, all I could mumble was, "Whatever." Cheri called Marilyn and asked if they could be there in the morning.

"They'll be there at nine," she said. "You get there whenever you want." Cheri hung up the phone. "That was God," she said to me.

I had to agree.

ON THE EDGE

As Cheri helped me to get dressed the next morning, she noticed that the side of the bed where my legs had been was soaking wet.

"Did you sit in something?" she asked.

We didn't think much more of it. When we got to the airport, we found that the plane's crew had fashioned a decent-sized bed out of two passenger seats. I sprawled out and slept nearly all the way home. When we landed in Dallas, Cheri's parents helped to unload me. Again, they noticed the bed was damp. Cheri called one of the doctors at Methodist and got an explanation.

"He's weeping. The body has taken in so much fluid it can't take any more, so the fluid is escaping from the pores."

It was not an encouraging sign. I spent a few days at home before my doctor visit on Monday. I was still "weeping," but at least I was back on my home turf. The downside was that I had work that I'd promised to do there, and my sense of duty hadn't deserted me. I had served as a spokesman for the James Wood chain of auto dealerships in the Dallas area for several years. They had asked me to complete a new commercial we'd begun before I got so sick. To my wife's dismay, I said I'd do it on the way to my doctor's appointment on Monday. After all, I wasn't quite fully incapacitated, I argued.

So on Monday, Cheri and the production people helped me to get dressed. It took a bit more makeup than usual to make me look present-able. Then they propped me up in front of the camera. We shot that video—quickly, thank God—and off I went to the doctor, who immedi-ately hospitalized me. I later learned that the folks at the dealership were so concerned about my appearance that morning that James Wood led his employees in praying for me.

They had good reason. The doctors again told Cheri I might have just hours to live.

They sent me to Methodist Hospital where I was admitted and began going downhill fast. My spirits were low. I felt I was going downhill each day. The staff tried more diuretics to get some of the fluids out of me, but had little success. Meanwhile, news of my illness was leaking out. Cheri and I wanted to make certain the information was accurate, so we worked up a press release. I also asked Cheri to contact columnist Frank Luksa of the *Dallas Morning News*, a longtime friend. Frank came to the hospital and was shaken when he saw me.

"I wasn't ready to see how sick he was," he told Cheri.

Still, he put up a good front, cracking jokes and trying to boost my spirits. We had a good visit, and he went back to work and wrote a won-derful story. But my story was about to get even more interesting.

NUMBER ONE

The next day, Cheri got a call from a nurse named Tiffany at the Mayo Clinic. All transplant centers do evaluations once a week in which they rate patients and their eligibility based on a variety of factors, including how close they are to death based on a national rating system called MELD (Modern End-Stage Liver Disease). It seemed I had moved up the list.

"Pat has been accepted into the program," Tiffany said.

Overwhelmed, Cheri started to cry, though she still didn't quite grasp what to do.

"Just tell us what we need to do," Cheri asked.

"Pat is so bad he is at the top of the list—nationally," Tiffany answered. "Just give us the okay and we'll make all the arrangements with the air ambulance."

It was the ultimate good-news-bad-news scenario. I was eligible for a life-saving transplant only because I was on the verge of death.

The ironies were all over us that day. It was April 1, which we always remembered as Mickey Mantle's favorite day of the year. We were hoping there were no pranks involved in this phone call.

They wanted us back in Jacksonville as soon as possible.

Cheri ran into my room, where I was conked out. She shook me and told me that I had been accepted at Mayo. I mumbled something. She took that for consent.

Then she started to make the arrangements to return to the Mayo Clinic in Jacksonville. As always, there were complications. Some doctors at Methodist fought Cheri on her decision to move me. They told her that it could very well kill me. Some even implied that she didn't know what she was doing. She was leaving the hospital to go home and pack our bags when a nurse ran after her and stopped her in a hallway.

Cheri had her dukes up. "What do you want now?"

"You're doing the right thing," the nurse assured her.

DASH FOR LIFE

Cheri rode with me in the medical vehicle to meet the emergency medical jet at Executive Airport. They loaded my bloated three-hundred-pound body on the small Lear jet, then packed in two medical attendants, two pilots, and an array of monitors and other equipment. Cheri had to squeeze into a corner, but there was no way they were leaving her behind. I think she would have ridden on the tail if necessary.

The attendants monitored and medicated me all the way to Jacksonville, and kept in constant radio communication with the Mayo staff. I was in excruciating pain! Every little rise and fall of the jet compounded my agony. I prayed to hold on to my fading hope. *Lord, get us through this.*

The three-hour trip felt like thirty hours inside a giant tumbling machine. My old body was giving out, but the old warrior in me fought to hang on. I was so still on the flight that Cheri reached over and touched my foot. She was relieved when I wiggled a toe, to signal that I was still on board. I faded in and out, but it did strike me that I was coming full circle. Soon I would be arriving at an airport that was just minutes away from my birthplace, Lake City. It also hit me that it would probably be good to die close to home.

There remained one huge "if" in the transplant equation. I was cleared for the operation if a donor liver could be found that matched my rare blood type. So, after the mad dash through the air to Jacksonville, the waiting began. Meanwhile, the hospital plied me with massive doses of Lasix and hooked me up to a dialysis machine to relieve my body of the built-up fluids. It worked. I still felt deathly ill, but some of the pressure was relieved. It didn't help that I could not get any extended sleep because of all the equipment hooked up to my failing body. If I dozed off for ten minutes, it was a moral victory. I was fighting and fighting, but getting discouraged.

"I am just so tired," I told my wife.

Cheri and my kids were doing their best not to let me lapse into despair. "We've come this far," she told me. "God's going to bring us through this." I told her, "If I could just feel good one more day."

My ammonia levels fluctuated wildly, and that caused me to babble at times. But for the most part, I kept a level head, though I remembered little—except for one overriding, tragic realization: It wasn't just my mortality at stake here. Someone would have to die so I could continue to live. How could I, or anyone, ask for that?

LIFELINE

As the days dragged by, it became tougher and tougher to stay positive. In the first few days they could not perform a transplant on me because I was in such bad shape. Donated organs are precious commodities, and surgeons do not want to give them to people who don't stand a very good chance of surviving the operation. We didn't grasp what was going on. We only knew that the clock was ticking, and my strength was fading. I had faith, but I was losing hope.

We had been in Jacksonville, waiting for the transplant, for eight days. The nurses were frantically trying to get the fluids out of me, and they were taking bag after bag off the dialysis machine, but I was still a hundred pounds over my normal weight. Every time a doctor or nurse walked into the room, we expected them to say it was time to prepare for surgery. We couldn't understand why it was taking so long. Cheri had watched me bloat into an unrecognizable blob. She'd married a pretty dapper guy, but now she was dealing with a three-hundred-pound invalid.

On Friday night, April 9, after the staff cleared visitors out for the night, Cheri finally lost it. She had done her best to be the cheerleader and the motivator, but the extended effort was wearing her down as well. My physical deterioration was tearing her up emotionally. She was sobbing by the time she reached the parking lot. She got to the car and collapsed inside, crying out to God, wondering what his plan was and why I was being put through so much suffering. Finally, she pulled herself together a little and began to drive through the parking lot. Through her tears, she saw red lights in the evening twilight and realized it was the landing field.

Something drew Cheri to the landing pad. She got out of the car and felt this odd sense of relief sweep over her. Raising her arms, she prayed, *God, we put Pat's fate in your loving hands.* She then turned and walked back to her car with a sense of peace. *Whatever happens, we are going to get through this,* she thought.

FAITH HEALS

That night, Cheri got the best sleep she'd gotten all week. She rose early that Saturday morning to get back to the hospital, and when she walked into my room she saw the sun streaming in the windows and a radiant smile on my bloated face.

I waited for her to kiss me hello before I broke the news.

"They have my liver," I said. "And they are prepping me for surgery."

As you might imagine, those words unleashed a river of tears from both of us. We must have been quite a sight, hugging and crying on my bed. Even the nurse joined in. I'm not sure hugging and crying with a patient and his wife is in the handbook, but she did a very fine job of sharing the moment.

Dr. Winston Hewitt, a member of Mayo's world-renowned liver transplant group, entered during the love fest and took it all in with a benevolent smile. "Mr. Summerall, I just got the most beautiful liver you've even seen. And it is for you."

It struck Cheri that she'd never before thought of a liver as a thing of beauty, but we both had to agree in this case, particularly when we understood what a gift it had been. My kids arrived, and they were overjoyed to hear the news, too.

Dr. Hewitt told us that the head surgeon would be in to see us in a little while, then turned to me and said, "We'll get you ready and probably go in about noon. And I just want you to know, I had the distinct privilege of harvesting your liver."

It hit us then. This truly was a miraculous gift. Our joy at finding a match was tempered by the realization that it had come only because another person had died. We said a prayer for the donor and his family, whose identity we did not know at that point. Our doctor said we had much to be thankful for.

"Pat, it is perfect," Dr. Hewitt said. "I believe God picked this just for you."

Cheri and the kids held hands around my bed and prayed. Just then, Dr. Jeffrey Steers, the head surgeon, walked in. He modestly offered his name, saying he didn't know if we remembered him. We assured him that we did. Dr. Jeffery Steers was surgical director of the Mayo Clinic and chairman of its Department of Transplantation. He is easily one of the best transplant surgeons in the world. (I'm living proof!)

Dr. Steers gave us the drill, so to speak, noting that the procedure would likely take four-and-a-half to five hours. As he talked, I saw him glance up at the television set in my room. The third round of the 2004 Masters was on that day.

"Do you like golf?" I asked.

He said he did, very much.

Cheri told him that she was sorry he'd miss watching the Masters during my operation. But I wanted to keep this guy in a good mood, for obvious reasons.

"Doc, I tell you what. You get me through this, I'll take you to Augusta—personally."

"Pat, I'm going to hold you to that!" he said.

IN GOD'S HANDS

I was in the operating room and the medical team was preparing for surgery when I shocked Dr. Steers by extending my hand to shake his before he went to work.

He looked at me very curiously.

"You're not supposed to be conscious for this," he said.

He motioned to the anesthesiologist to give me a little more juice. Then we shook.

"Doc, I'm in your hands," I said.

"No, Pat, we are both in God's hands," he replied.

While I was on the table, I dreamed of being in a big, cold room in Minnesota, arguing with doctors about how they were going to proceed. I felt myself getting smaller and smaller, until I was nothing but the end of a tailbone. I wondered, *Is this what it's like to die? You just shrink away to nothing?*

In my dream, I lost the argument with the doctors. They left the room one by one. I was shivering uncontrollably. But I felt the presence of another figure in the room—a man standing in the corner. He brought over a big, gray blanket and gently pulled it over me.

"This will keep you warm," he said in a reassuring voice.

I warmed up instantly, then closed my eyes for just a second. I opened them with a start when I realized who the man was: It was Jesus Christ! I had just seen Christ, and I hadn't even tried to talk with him. You'd think after all those years as a network broadcaster, I could have thought of a couple of quick questions for the Son of God.

Two-and-a-half hours later, Cheri was startled to see Dr. Steers and fellow transplant surgeon Dr. Darrin Willingham walk into the surgical unit waiting room.

It is too early! Something must have gone wrong, she thought.

Reading her face, Dr. Steers spoke out to reassure her: "No, no, no. Everything's fine, it's fine. Everything's great, I assure you."

It had gone like clockwork, the surgeon said.

"I can't tell you how perfect it was," he added. "That's a record time!"

Miraculously, there were no complications. Before surgery, the doctors had warned Cheri that there would be a tube sticking out of my side when they brought me out. It would go into my bile duct, and they were going to put dye in there to check my progress for a couple of weeks during recovery. I would also be on a ventilator, they'd told her.

When they wheeled me into my room, I awoke with the ventilator in place, and in my confused state, I panicked. It was a common post-op reaction; the nurses had to secure my arms to the side. My reaction upset Cheri and the kids. Meanwhile, Cheri was frantically searching for that big bile-duct tube that was supposed to be protruding from me. She looked under the covers, underneath me—everywhere. Just then, Dr. Willingham came in and saw she was panicked.

"Where is that tube that's supposed to be in his side?" she asked.

"There's nothing wrong. The liver was such a perfect match, it didn't have to be done," Dr. Willingham said.

I didn't mind it at all when folks around the Mayo Clinic began referring to me as "the perfect transplant."

CHAPTER THIRTEEN

POST-PERFECT TRANSPLANT

JUST WHEN I WAS GETTING A LITTLE COCKY ABOUT BEING SUCH A "perfect" transplant patient, I got the upsetting news that my doctors wanted to take me back into surgery for a little clean-up. My blood count had not gone up like it was supposed to after the transplant, so they feared there might a little bleeding somewhere, which was not unusual. I was less than thrilled and I let them know it. But they convinced me that it was better safe than sorry. As it turned out, they found no major problems, and as soon as they cleaned me out and sewed me back up my blood count started improving just like the doctor ordered. The worst of it was that I missed watching the final round of the Masters Tournament when Phil Mickelson made the winning putt.

Still, I cruised through the rest of the week, amazing my doctors, family, and friends with my recuperative powers.

Then, without warning, I went berserk.

Cheri and I had been doing devotions every morning, and it was something I looked forward to. We began reading Bible passages from Ezekiel, which I'd always found interesting, but on that Friday morning I couldn't concentrate. I was irritable and restless. My reputation as the hospital's Mr. Congeniality was in serious jeopardy. When the physical therapy team came in, I refused to get out of bed for them. The staff gave me a wide berth for the rest of the day, figuring that I was just having a cranky day.

As grateful as I was for the miracle of the perfect match and the success of the transplant operation, I was worn out. I had slept very little over the previous five weeks because I was in so much pain. Even in the hospital, I didn't get much rest because of the constant coming and going of nurses and other staff checking on me, prodding and poking me throughout the night. Dr. May had warned us that fatigue combined with the effects of the antirejection medication sometimes causes patients to act erratically after a transplant operation.

When I got so irritable, my caregivers saw what was happening, and they made Cheri and all other visitors clear out at 6:30 p.m. so I could get some rest. Cheri wanted to come back at 9 p.m. to say good night, but I told her not to bother. I thought she needed a full night's sleep, too. She left, saying she was going to get things ready at a condo she'd rented for my release from the hospital.

BAD PAT

Cheri was awakened at 12:30 a.m. by a call from the nursing staff. Mr. Congeniality had turned into Frankenstein. "He won't take his medication and he's saying he wants to leave now," the night nurse said.

Cheri came a-running. She found me lying in my dimly lit room. I told her I felt weird and uneasy. She told me I had to stay strong like Ezekiel and fight. We were nearly done with this trial, she said. I agreed. She said she'd stay with me. She rubbed my arm, and taking comfort in her presence, I drifted off.

Cheri waited until I was asleep then tiptoed out, telling the nurse that she was going back to the condo to get some sleep.

At 3 a.m. her phone rang again. "Pat is having a screaming fit, and he's fighting to leave the hospital. He's demanding to see you!" the night nurse said.

Poor Cheri scrambled back to the hospital where she found me sitting up in the bed with all the lights on. My wife had lost her patience with my antics.

"Pat, what is wrong with you?"

It may have been a rhetorical question, but she got a literal answer. "What do you think is wrong with me? My lips just fell off! Quick, grab my arm—it's going, too. And my leg!"

Shocked, Cheri stepped back from my bed. I was wild-eyed, frantic, and totally out of my gourd.

"He's been doing this and screaming for you," said the nurse.

I looked at Cheri with glazed eyes and issued a new command: "Quick! Grab Roscoe before he falls off!"

"Who the heck is Roscoe?" Cheri said.

"Don't act like you don't know who Roscoe is," I said, pointing at my crotch. "You know exactly who Roscoe is."

That left Cheri speechless, so I apparently decided to fill the conversational gap by screaming again that my lips, arms, legs, and yes, Roscoe, too, were falling off.

Then I went silent, gave Cheri a wild stare, and issued yet another off-the-wall command: "I don't want to hear any more of that Ezekiel @%!& either!"

Cheri gave in to the insanity.

"Okay, babe, you got it!" she said.

At that point, she was thinking, *I want my husband back.*

LOOSE LIPS

It was as if I'd been possessed. I was relentless, demanding that she get me out of there because "they" were going to kill me. I demanded that she call Jerry Jones and get him to send the plane to take us back to Dallas.

Cheri stopped fighting it and played along, telling me that she'd called Jerry and there was a terrible storm in Dallas so the plane couldn't get out of the airport.

I started cursing and screaming at that report. Nurses came running from all directions. I was still in the intensive care unit, and I was disturbing the other patients. They told Cheri that patients on antirejection medication sometimes had these psychotic episodes if they didn't get enough sleep. I was definitely in my own orbit.

I was working up a fury, screaming that they were going to kill me. I demanded that Cheri call my daughter, Susan, because she had influence with the city government in Jacksonville.

Instead, Cheri asked the nurses to summon Dr. Mai, who was on call. It was about 5:30 a.m. Cheri was afraid that I was headed for a crash because I wouldn't take my antirejection medication.

Dr. Mai walked in coolly and calmly.

"Is there a problem?" he asked.

He got an immediate and adamant response.

"What do you think? My lips fell off! I make a living talking. How am I going to talk with no lips?"

Dr. Mai looked at Cheri and said, "Remember, I told you that sometimes we see this in transplant patients during recovery."

"Yeah, but this is scary," said Cheri.

"We'll be fine," the doctor said.

"You may be okay, but I don't know who that man is in the bed," Cheri replied.

I was then inspired to offer a totally unrehearsed a cappella medley of "God Bless America" and "Amazing Grace"—at the top of my lungs: live in the intensive care unit.

You've never seen nurses move a man out of an ICU so quickly. They may have set a world speed record for transporting a body on a bed with wheels. Suddenly, they had room for me on the transplant floor, which had been too crowded earlier. Later I learned they got sneaky by crushing up my antirejection medication and putting it in my fruit juice.

GONE IN A FLASH

Kyle came to see me early that morning, around 7:30. The doctor told him of my Jekyll-Hyde impersonation, and requested that family members take turns staying with me around the clock to help deal with "Bad Pat." The doctors eliminated Cheri from the family rotation, saying that if she didn't get some rest, there might be two monsters in the recovery unit.

It was a Saturday, so Kyle and Susan decided to trade off between tending to their own families. Cheri was sent home to sleep. Susan volunteered for the first shift, though I was still in full roar. Bad Pat immediately turned on her, reaming her out for keeping him hostage in the hospital. Worried about my prolonged personality shift, the staff called in another physician for a consult. It was Dr. Lee, whose daughter is a friend of Susan's. They exchange pleasantries as I glared at them like Linda Blair in *The Exorcist* before the priest cleaned up her act.

After talking briefly with Susan, Dr. Lee turned to me and asked what seemed to be the problem. "What do you think? My arms and lips and legs are falling off, and now they've sent a Chinaman into my room!"

Susan wanted to crawl under the nearest bedpan and hide. She fled the room and stayed outside, where the staff assured her that her father had not turned into Don Rickles's evil twin. I had managed to insult or offend nearly everyone within the Mayo zip code in a very small amount of time.

While Susan was still in the hallway seeking relief from my madness, she looked up to see the exposed rear end of her deranged father hobbling down the hall in the opposite direction. My hospital gown—and everything else—was flapping in the wind. To complete my escape ensemble, I had wrapped a towel into a turban around my head and was dragging my catheter bag as an accessory.

"Dad, what are you doing?" Susan shouted at my bared backside.

"Shhh! I'm getting out of here before they kill me!" I replied.

The hospital staff wrestled me back to the room before I was able to flash Jacksonville's entire east side.

DIE HARD, SR.

At that, Susan surrendered. She called Kyle and said, "I can't do this. It is too much."

They gave me sedatives, but they weren't having much effect. Cheri called in early to check on me, but they refused to tell her the truth, wisely. Kyle had spent the night listening to me scream for Jerry Jones and his airplane. Then it got weirder.

Cheri couldn't get back to sleep so she came to the hospital around 6:00 a.m. and found Kyle talking to a doctor in the hallway. As she approached them, she noticed Kyle's black shirt was covered with hairs that were a familiar shade of gray.

"Now what did he do?" my wife asked my son.

"Dad got hold of an electric razor and started hacking his hair off before I could wrestle it away from him," Kyle said. "He is still strong as an ox."

Cheri walked in and saw that I'd managed to shear down to the scalp in a number of places.

"Pat, what in the world made you do that?"

"I wanted to look like Bruce Willis!" I told her.

"Why?"

"I thought I was going to die."

Cheri noted that I still wasn't making much sense, but I had mellowed considerably. I still wanted to leave, but I was no longer demanding that the plane land in the parking lot immediately.

"Did you ever get hold of Jerry Jones?" I asked.

"No, Jerry's not coming and you are staying here," Cheri said.

"Oh, I thought we were going to leave," I said.

I'd moved into a more passive state, but the thrill ride wasn't over. A few minutes later, after helping me into the bathroom, Cheri discovered that I'd found some scissors and I was back to playing Bruce Willis's barber. My wife took the scissors away and chastised me like a child, which was appropriate given my behavior.

As the day progressed, my disposition was sunnier with occasional clouds of confusion. I had no memory of cutting my hair or streaking down the hallway. You know it was bad when members of the nursing staff check in to say they prayed for you all night while they were off duty.

My wife and children spent most of Sunday recovering from my antics. Susan checked in on me Monday morning before going to work. She then called Cheri at her condo to offer her assessment. "He seems to be getting back to normal, but when I went to kiss him good-bye, he said, 'Before you leave, just hand me my other set of lips, would you? I can't eat breakfast without them.'"

CHAPTER FOURTEEN

AMEN CORNER

MY BRIEF BOUT OF CRAZINESS WAS THE ONLY HITCH IN MY RECOVERY from the transplant operation. My body showed no signs of rejecting the new liver; so once "Bad Pat" faded, good Pat went home. The transplant was a blessing that brought great joy and relief to my family and me. Yet I often reflected on the fact that it came at the cost of another life, and I wondered about the donor and those he loved.

We were not given any information about the donor, but because of all the talk of a "perfect match," I'd envisioned that it was a man around my size. I thought of his loved ones mourning even as mine were overjoyed at my second chance at life. I also had pangs of guilt about getting the donor's healthy organ after I had destroyed my own. I'd been given so many blessings, but I had screwed it up royally with my drinking. Worst of all, I had hurt those I loved deeply.

I kept wondering why I'd been given this second chance, while the donor had died. I looked for answers from my church minister and friends. Their responses were remarkably similar: "God's not through with you yet. You've got a lot of work to do. You can help other people."

Still, I told my friend John Weber, I was struggling with the fact that someone had to die for me to live. Always wise, he corrected me. "Pat isn't that exactly what Jesus Christ did for all of us?"

I felt a sense of peace for the first time. John's words helped put things in a better perspective for me.

But what was it that God had in store for me? In some ways, I was a good example of a bad example. Mine had not exactly been an exemplary life. My hard-earned achievements in sports and broadcasting were accompanied by personal failings: the neglect of my family, my health, and my relationship with God. Whatever my remaining missions might be, I had a lot of catching up to do.

I felt responsible for making good on two lives after my transplant. I offered to speak for organ donation causes, in hopes of repaying my donor and encouraging others. And I began speaking wherever I could to spread the miracle of faith that had blessed my life. God willing, I intend to follow Christ's teachings and help as many people as I can.

DEAR DONOR

Six months after my transplant, it was suggested that I write a letter to the liver donor's family to express my gratitude. In it, I told them of the joys I had experienced in my "second" life, and of all of the things I would have missed if I hadn't received the transplanted liver. I thanked the family for their compassion. I couldn't tell them who I was or what I did. That was part of the confidential nature of the process. If the family wanted to get in touch with me, they would. I was told that most often, they don't.

It was a very, very difficult letter to write. It kept hitting me that, no matter what I said or how I said it, there was no way to ease their grief. They had lost a loved one. How could I ease that heartache? Over the years, my voice had reached millions and millions of people that I could not see. Now, I struggled to communicate with these few strangers who had saved my life.

I have experienced many blessings in this "extra" time. I was even given the opportunity to return to the broadcast booth, to prove that I could still engage sports' fans. Less than four months after my surgery, I was contacted by ESPN in early August. They were looking for help because their Sunday Night NFL broadcast crew was temporarily short a man. Play-by-play pro Mike Patrick had taken a stress test after feeling ill following a golf game.

It was a good thing he took the test. The hospital admitted him for triple-bypass surgery. He hadn't suffered a heart attack, but he was headed for one.

An ESPN producer asked if I could sub for Mike for the final four games of the exhibition season. I wasn't sure that I was quite up to the task, and my family members and caregivers were apprehensive as well. Many liver transplant patients my age have no desire to return to stressful jobs. But I loved my work, and I was growing bored without it. I went to Mayo for a checkup, and they cleared me for take-off. I worried that I might not have the strength for it, but the doctors and staff seemed to think I could handle it—as long as my lips didn't fall off during the game.

It helped my confidence that ESPN teamed me with a couple of pros. Veteran analysts Joe Theismann and Paul Maguire were very protective of their temp worker. After the newness wore off, we relaxed and just had fun. It felt so good being back on the air that I didn't want it to end. The fans seemed to enjoy it, too. We received bundles of encouraging letters, and I was touched by the supportive messages about my treatment for alcoholism and reborn faith. It had gone so well, in fact, that ESPN asked me to stay on for four regular-season games while Mike Patrick recuperated. It was great to get a chance to prove that I could still do the job at that level.

This second chance at life has been sweet in many ways. I especially enjoyed returning to Augusta National, courtesy of my friend Joe Ford, a member of Augusta, who hosted me and Dr. Steers, my transplant surgeon, and sharing the beauty of my favorite place with him. I'd watched the 2004 Masters from my hospital bed at the Mayo Clinic, and at the time I wasn't sure that I would ever make it back. Chris Schenkel and I were the only two people to be given gold badges that allowed us to play Augusta any time we wanted. They had been a gift from Masters' chairman Jack Stephens, the same fellow from Arkansas who gave me my first winter coat. I was always grateful for the opportunity to play Augusta, but Amen Corner has taken on a whole new significance for me now.

RETURNING A FAVOR

In March of 2005, Arkansas governor Mike Huckabee asked me to serve as the keynote speaker at a luncheon honoring organ-donor families. It was put on by the state organization that provides transplant organs to people like me—the Arkansas Regional Organ Recovery Agency (ARORA). I agreed to do it even before one of the organizers told Cheri that they were excited to have me speak at the event, "especially since his liver came from Arkansas."

So it seemed that I'd forged yet another link to the state where I'd spent my college years and formed so many lasting friendships.

As we prepared for the Arkansas event, we learned through the state's organ recovery folks that the family of my liver donor had not yet read my letter. We understood their grief. The fact that they might be in the audience for my "Gift of Life" speech at the governor's mansion was intimidating. It was also true that many brothers, sisters, mothers, and fathers of organ donors would be present. No matter how upbeat this event was, it would still rekindle heartbreaking memories and powerful emotions. Again, I had qualms.

I'll be standing there in front of them, as a recovering alcoholic who had abused his own body. How could I talk about my good fortune at receiving a transplant, which was possible only because of the death of one of their loved ones?

I was afraid of coming off as callous and self-centered to people I'd imagined were carrying tremendous grief in their hearts. So, in giving my speech to the more than five hundred people who came to the luncheon at the governor's mansion, I kept it simple. I thanked them for their compassion, for saving not just my life but also hundreds of others, and I made a point of directing thanks especially to whoever had provided my own donated organ. Then, after my speech, I spent a very rewarding evening talking one on one with family members who, while saddened by the loss of loved ones, were heartened by the fact that other lives had been saved or made better. It was such a relief.

A CHILD LOST

A few months after my speech to the Arkansas organ donors, our contacts in the state's organ recovery program notified me that my donor's family had expressed an interest in meeting me. They had signed release forms to allow contact. The program staff members wanted to get us together to meet for healing purposes.

The family was from Pine Bluff. The mother's name was Melva Shelby. The father's name was Garland. And their son, my donor, was named Adron.

We were astonished to learn that Adron had died at the age of thirteen. He was just a student in junior high school when he collapsed while giving a speech in history class. He died three days later of a brain aneurysm. During the effort to keep him alive, some of Adron's organs were damaged, but the family donated his eyes, liver, and kidneys. A few days after I received their precious gift, the Shelbys buried their son.

When Cheri heard the details of Adron's age and the circumstances of his death, she was overwhelmed. It took her a few minutes to recover from the emotional impact. She then gathered herself and came to my reading room to tell me. It triggered powerful emotions in me, too. I kept thinking of my thirteen-year-old granddaughter, so young and full of promise. I couldn't imagine how the family dealt with his death, or the decision to donate his organs. Above all, I didn't know how they would feel when they met me. I was so much older. I had lived so much longer.

We were still dealing with the information about Adron a few weeks later when Natalie, a staffer with the Arkansas organ recovery program, called and said that my donor's mother wanted to speak on the telephone to Cheri.

Why me? Cheri thought.

Apparently, Melva had done some research and found stories about me, including things that Cheri had said during my illness and after the transplant. Melva had been impressed that we were Christians, and she thought she and Cheri might be able to talk easier as women.

They talked for forty-five minutes, though Cheri said it was one of the most heartwrenching conversations she ever experienced. Melva quoted Scripture, but she asked some tough questions of Cheri to test our commitment to our faith. We could see that in her grief, Melva wanted the comfort of knowing that her son's gift had gone to a worthy person.

"They say your husband is famous," Melva said to her. "They say he is a celebrity."

"It's true we are blessed in many ways," Cheri said.

She noted that because of my career in broadcasting, I often spoke to large groups and to the media. Cheri told my donor's mother that I often used those forums to thank her family for what they had done.

"Now, when Pat stands up in front of all these people to thank your family, his donor will have a name and, hopefully, a picture. Your son will be honored," Cheri said. "I know that won't bring him back, Melva, and it doesn't help with the pain. But this is a way to memorialize him."

A BETTER LIFE

Melva was moved, and she asked to meet with us. Cheri set a date for August 10, 2005, which was seventeen months to the day after I received the liver. Both Cheri and I were on edge as that meeting date approached. I'd been nervous enough when I spoke to the Arkansas donor families. But now, I would be meeting the donor's family face-to-face.

I struggled to think of the right words, words that would convey my gratitude and respect without renewing their heartache. I had spent forty-five years as a broadcaster and had called sixteen Super Bowls. Rarely did I worry about making the right call at the right time—and I never lacked for words when other media approached me. This was different.

I was stymied. I had no idea what I was going to say to this family when we met them in Little Rock. *What could I say?* I wondered. Somehow, "Thank you. You saved my life. God bless you," just didn't seem adequate.

I had given considerable thought to the fact that a donated organ was the most precious of gifts. It had caused me to reflect more deeply on my life than I ever had. Those reflections inspired me to strengthen my own family bonds. Adron's gift not only gave me more life, it changed my perspective on life for the better.

HEALING GRACE

I had those thoughts in mind as we boarded our plane for the short trip to Little Rock. It would probably have been much better had we conducted our entire meeting in private, but the Arkansas organ donor program had arranged for us to first meet privately and then to stage a press conference to increase organ-donation awareness. Their goal was to save more lives, and we certainly supported their cause.

The minute we walked into the room, Melva spotted Cheri, approached her, and hugged her. Then she hugged me. I talked to her from my heart, and thanked her and her family. I expressed condolences for the loss of her son, and I told her what a difference their organ-donation decision had made in not only keeping me alive but making me a better person.

She hugged me again and said, "It's almost like I'm hugging a part of my child."

To my relief, the meeting with Adron's family—and there was an impressive contingent of them present—became a very upbeat and exhilarating experience. The press conference made national news, and the news magazine show *Nightline* did a story as well, so it helped a life-saving cause.

Most importantly, it was a healing experience for Adron's family. His brother Chan had been depressed and withdrawn prior to the meeting, but by day's end he was smiling and even laughing. "This has done more for him than anything," Melva told us. "It was a good feeling, knowing we helped so many other people. Adron's memory lives on, and now so does his name."

I'm determined to honor the memory of Adron Shelby by living up to his promise as a young man of integrity and faith. I am, after all, "young" in a couple respects. I have his liver, which has been a miraculous gift, and I am young also in my Christian rebirth and God's wonderful redeeming grace.

As you might recall, I entered this world a little twisted, and it took a while longer than anticipated to get me completely straightened out. Yet anyone familiar with all aspects of my life needs no other proof; I am a living testament to the undeniable fact that God's grace is utterly and completely boundless.

> "*T'was Grace that taught my heart to fear,*
> *and Grace, my fears relieved.*
> *How precious did that Grace appear*
> *the hour I first believed . . .*"

ACKNOWLEDGMENTS

I'D LIKE TO SAY THANK YOU TO THE PUBLISHERS, TO JAN MILLER, TO STEVE McLinden, and especially Wes Smith, who listened and wrote. And to all those family and friends in the book who helped me create these memories of what has been a wonderfully blessed life.

And to my Lord, who guided me always even if I didn't always know who was talking.

To learn more about organ transplantation
and how you have the power to save lives visit:

www.unos.org

www.donatelife.net

CPSIA information can be obtained at www.ICGtesting.com
Printed in the USA
LVOW041215061212

310400LV00001B/52/P